FROM INTERVENTION TO SOCIAL CHANGE

T0362339

Solving Social Problems

Series Editor:
Bonnie Berry, Director of the Social Problems Research Group, USA

Solving Social Problems provides a forum for the description and measurement of social problems, with a keen focus on the concrete remedies proposed for their solution. The series takes an international perspective, exploring social problems in various parts of the world, with the central concern being always their possible remedy. As such, work is welcomed on subjects as diverse as environmental damage, terrorism, economic disparities and economic devastation, poverty, inequalities, domestic assaults and sexual abuse, health care, natural disasters, labour inequality, animal abuse, crime, and mental illness and its treatment. In addition to recommending solutions to social problems, the books in this series are theoretically sophisticated, exploring previous discussions of the issues in question, examining other attempts to resolve them, and adopting and discussing methodologies that are commonly used to measure social problems. Proposed solutions may be framed as changes in policy, practice, or more broadly, social change and social movement. Solutions may be reflective of ideology, but are always pragmatic and detailed, explaining the means by which the suggested solutions might be achieved.

Also in the series

Preventing Human Trafficking
Education and NGOs in Thailand
Robert W. Spires

Service Sociology and Academic Engagement in Social Problems
Edited by A. Javier Treviño and Karen M. McCormack

Women, Incarceration, and Human Rights Violations
Feminist Criminology and Corrections
Alana Van Gundy and Amy Baumann-Grau

Regulating Alcohol around the World
Policy Cocktails
Tiffany Bergin

From Intervention to Social Change
A Guide to Reshaping Everyday Practices

TRIIN VIHALEMM, MARGIT KELLER AND MAIE KIISEL
University of Tartu, Estonia

Routledge
Taylor & Francis Group

LONDON AND NEW YORK

First published 2015 by Ashgate Publishing

2 Park Square, Milton Park, Abingdon, Oxfordshire OX14 4RN
52 Vanderbilt Avenue, New York, NY 10017

Routledge is an imprint of the Taylor & Francis Group, an informa business

First issued in paperback 2020

British Library Cataloguing in Publication Data
A catalogue record for this book is available from the British Library

The Library of Congress has cataloged the printed edition as follows:
Vihalemm, Triin, 1968–
  From intervention to social change : a guide to reshaping everyday practices / by Triin Vihalemm, Margit Keller and Maie Kiisel.
    pages cm.—(Solving social problems)
  Includes bibliographical references and index.
  ISBN 978-1-4724-5190-3 (hardback)
1. Social problems. 2. Social action. 3. Social change. 4. Social policy. I. Title.
  HN18.3.V54 2015
  303.3—dc23

2015000867

ISBN 978-1-4724-5190-3 (hbk)
ISBN 978-0-367-59849-5 (pbk)

Contents

List of Figures and Tables

Figures

Tables

Acknowledgements

In writing this book, the three authors did not walk alone. There were many companions we wish to thank most warmly: our colleague at the University of Tartu, Kadri Ugur, for giving constructive feedback, especially about the didactic aspects of the book; the master's students in communication management and medicine at the University of Tartu, on whom we tried out the earlier versions of the book; the international students from various disciplines at the University of Helsinki, who gave valuable feedback; and the local programme manager, Yonca Ermutlu, who helped us to arrange the courses.

Bente Halkier, Alan Warde, Terhi-Anna Wilska, Tally Katz-Gerro, Lydia Marters, Olga Kravets, Dale Southerton, Monica Truninger, Lotte Holm, Eivind Stø, Jukka Gronow, Michael Egerer, Irmak Karademir Hazir and Pekka Sulkunen deserve our deep gratitude for inspiring us to become involved in practice theory and providing examples of excellent analyses through their articles, books, conference presentations and, above all, friendly collegial support. The Sociology of Consumption Research Network of the European Sociological Association has been an international family for Margit Keller, who has had the honour of chairing this network for a few years. Its conferences have sparked many ideas that made this book possible.

We also wish to express our gratitude to numerous professionals at Estonian public institutions and civic organisations who have provided interesting data and projects to consult, work on and analyse: Viola Murd and Janek Innos at the Estonian Rescue Board, Hanna Turetski at the Consumer Protection Agency, Leonore Riitsalu and Heli Lehtsaar at the Estonian Financial Supervision Authority, Lauri Tammiste and Tanel Liiv at the Estonian Environmental Investment Centre and Rasmus Pedanik from the Social Innovation Network. We thank our students and members of our social practices research unit for their contribution in investigating various social change programmes and projects, and colleagues at the Institute of Social Studies of the University of Tartu for their inspiring questions and interest.

Our gratitude is due to Richard Adang, our English language editor, for his careful work. The artists Tanel Rannala and Siiri Taimla from Joonmeedia have brought the book to life with many original hand-drawings, which are an integral part of this book's message. We would also like to thank Springtime industrial design BV, Reet Ruusmann and Anu Järs from the Estonian National Museum and Helgi Põllo and Urmas Liit from Hiiumaa Museum and our friends Helen Ennok and Aare Abrams who helped us with photographs.

Ashgate's editors Neil Jordan and Sadie Copley-May have always been positive and provided quick feedback.

The writing of the book has been funded by two research grants: IUT 20–38 and ETF9017 from the Estonian Research Agency.

Preface

This book was mainly born out of the authors' inspiration from a rapidly emerging and very intriguing strand of sociological thinking called theories of social practices, and out of disenchantment with individual-centred public awareness campaigns that ambitiously strive to transform behaviours and affect social change. According to the *Encyclopaedia Britannica*, 'Social change' (n.d.) is 'the alteration of mechanisms within the social structure, characterized by changes in cultural symbols, rules of behaviour, social organizations, or value systems'. Contemporary societies in various parts of the world abound in projects and programmes which attempt to effect change, to transform society, to make people think and act differently: in a healthier, more sustainable, innovative, responsible and capable way. We can think of such initiatives and interventions into people's everyday lifestyles as 'social change programmes', which assume that social change can be galvanised and pushed in the desired direction if people are organised and make concerted efforts.

This book is written to help design, communicate and carry out programmes aimed at solving various problems: from reducing health-risk behaviour to 'green' or financially literate decisions. We concentrate on areas that are related to people's *lifestyles* and *consumption*. This book is meant for all those who at some point in their lives discover that they need to make a contribution to changing people's lifestyles and ways of consuming. We invite NGO project managers, social entrepreneurs and designers of public services, civic activists and volunteers, as well as governmental policy makers and officials who design, implement or evaluate projects meant to make people think and behave differently, to read this book.

We do not concentrate on one-off awareness campaigns, although examples of these are given in the book. This book aims to offer a social-theory-driven, step-by-step guide for practitioners on how to make projects effect lasting changes in people's consumption habits and everyday activities. It combines practical suggestions with academic discussion inspired by theories of social practices. This theoretical approach suggests new ways of making sense of things, including the routines of programme and campaign making.

One of the primary problems with present-day interventions is the relationship between the *sustainability of change* and *resources spent*: large investments are made, yet for a change to last even more resources – money, time, energy and human effort – are required. We believe that, to a great extent, this is due to the simplifying and universalising conceptions underlying those programmes. This book aims to offer a theoretically and empirically supported, *context-sensitive* treatment of the topic of social change programmes, supplemented with accessible and user-friendly *guidance* on programme planning, design and evaluation. We particularly focus on readers who may not have substantial financial and human resources at their disposal and who act in changing contexts. The book intends to be down-to-earth, usable and practitioner friendly, yet theory inspired and context sensitive.

Our textbook has four intended outcomes. We hope that after completing the book the reader will:

1. analyse the *everyday practices* of target audiences and stakeholders *and the social issues arising from such practices*, moving away from computer screens and plunging into real-life experience and fieldwork. For this purpose, we have included questions for reflection, and smaller and more difficult assignments (which we call Think and Stretch, aiming to convey the idea of expanding one's mind and thinking outside the box, as well as the necessity of fighting against a sedentary lifestyle), with references for further reading;

2. co-operate with stakeholders and beneficiaries so *that programmes will be co-creations*, not just guides to life imposed by experts on those who need help. The ethos of the book is that all such programmes benefit from being participatory, i.e., engaging their beneficiaries as *active citizens capable of social innovation*. The book explicitly focuses on citizens and citizen-consumers, not treating stakeholders as merely recipients of 'products' (passive consumers) designed to intervene in their lives;

3. build *coalitions* with other organisations dealing with similar issues, not treating them as competitors but as partners. This is crucial for several reasons. Firstly, making concerted and synergetic efforts decreases the *information overload* of audiences. Secondly, in order to bring about actual and lasting change, the involvement of various parties, from legislators to manufacturers, is often required. For example, actual practice change requires adapting the built environment, revising legislation and raising awareness, and not just focusing on the latter;

4. understand communication as a *powerful socio-material process* in which not only words and pictures, but also activities, material objects and environments shape emergent meanings. Communication is present in all actions and steps of the programme, and meaning is created even if no conscious communication management effort is made by 'communication specialists'.

The book consists of five chapters. Chapter 1 focuses on bridge-building and gives an overview of the basic categories: the main actors in the field and their specific concerns, and the main types of intervention. It positions the social practice theory-based approach in a wider conceptual landscape of individual behaviour change, social marketing and behavioural economics, and offers user-friendly guidance on manoeuvring between competing approaches. The authors' applied and academic experience has convinced us that decision-makers are often educated in instrumental and individualist concepts and models. We set out to provide tools that build bridges between views, and compare and discuss their (dis)advantages in a useful manner so that practitioners can position themselves and defend their ideas.

Chapter 2 focuses on the thriving area of social theory: theories of social practice. We explain Anthony Giddens's structuration theory in an accessible way, as well as examining some concepts of Pierre Bourdieu's theory of social fields. The chapter also compares the practice-based approach with individual behaviour change approaches, helping to establish a theoretical basis for understanding the dynamics and elements of social change at the micro level, and preparing the foundation for designing a change programme that is socially informed. Theoretical statements are illustrated by practical examples, along with information that will help to create an action programme. In Chapter 3, we move on to theory-driven aspects of how to apply seemingly complicated concepts in real-life social change programme design. The reader learns how to analyse practices and to set objectives of a programme. All suggestions and explanations are illustrated with brief examples from the authors' original research or from secondary sources. Chapter 4 deals with the preparation and implementation of an actual activity programme in which methods to be used in a programme are structured according to the elements of social practices: meanings, skills and things (see Shove, Pantzar and Watson, 2012). Chapter 5 focuses on how the practitioner can determine whether a programme is on track and how to collect feedback and data to evaluate the results of the programme. The book ends with Chapter 6, a 'tool-kit' containing questions and recommendations for each stage of a social change programme. The brief tool-kit is meant to assist the reader in planning, implementing and monitoring an actual work process, as well as performing subsequent evaluation. Finally, the book contains ample illustrations, most of which are original drawings made for this volume. We invite the reader to study and enjoy.

Chapter 1
Actors and ways of intervention

This chapter deals with the concept of social change programmes. We discuss some of the background of the theoretical and political issues entailed in attempts to solve lifestyle-related problems. Next, we introduce different actors, such as policy makers, market enterprises and civil society organisations, the main players who launch various interventions into consumers' and citizens' lives. After that, we juxtapose competing approaches (mainly individual-based social marketing and behavioural economics, including 'Nudge') with practice-change conceptualisation, although a more detailed discussion of the latter takes place in Chapter 2. The aim is to give programme designers a basic map of the field, in terms of concepts and actors, which will help them to position themselves.

1.1 Lifestyles and social change programmes

Alcohol and tobacco abuse, irresponsible driving styles, drugs, unhealthy nutrition, food risks, drowning, fire deaths, non-sustainable energy use, accumulation of waste and personal financial incapability: these are just a few examples of the social problems connected to modern lifestyles. These problems affect all members of society, not only risk groups. Alcohol abuse affects the welfare of a society and is a drain on our tax revenue. It is society as a whole that benefits, directly or indirectly, from attempts to alleviate or solve these problems.

This guidebook focuses on programmes that aim to *initiate social change* by making population groups think and act differently in order to improve the welfare of these groups and society as a whole. There is no agreed-upon common label either for such programmes or for related policies. Decades ago social scientists used the term *life politics* (Giddens, 1991; Roos and Hoikkala, 1998). This was defined by the well-known British sociologist Anthony Giddens (1991):

> While emancipatory politics is a politics of life chances, life politics is a politics of lifestyle. Life politics is the politics of a reflexively mobilised order – the system of late modernity – which, on an individual and collective level, has radically altered the existential parameters of social activity. It is a politics of self-actualisation in a reflexively ordered environment, where that reflexivity links self and body to systems of global scope … Life politics concerns political issues which flow from processes of self-actualisation in post-traditional contexts, where globalising influences intrude deeply into the reflexive project

of the self, and conversely where processes of self-realisation influence global strategies (p. 214).

In our book, we build on that definition, while focusing on policy-making and actual programme design useful in tackling 'lifestyle problems'. Thus we deal mainly with a set of political, economic, cultural and social tools implemented to shape, directly or indirectly, how people go about their own lives, as well as influencing other lives and social structures.[1]

These interventions are based on the assumption that, unlike traditional societies, in the contemporary era consumers' and citizens' abilities and opportunities to make (informed) choices and to consider the long-term consequences (pertaining to the natural environment, health, the wider social good etc.) of their actions have increased due to various socio-technological developments. Moreover, the lifestyles exercised, adopted and abandoned by the (general) population are believed to be the keys that open the door to further social prosperity. For example, many sustainable and innovative approaches to energy production and consumption struggle with the 'consumer factor', so that engineers and life scientists are waiting for answers from social scientists on how to educate the 'proper consumer'. Jeja-Pekka Roos, referring to Giddens (Roos, n.d.), has defined this as 'a new moral basis for existence in a situation where people have choices, resources and risks' and she states that they should develop new ethics concerning the issue of 'how we should live in a post-traditional order'. Giddens's ideas are further explored in Chapter 2.

Many classical social theorists and contemporary researchers are very sceptical about this approach and say that it is impossible to talk only about individual choices or decisions, as they are deeply entrenched in social power structures. Explanations are sought regarding how individual agents interrelate with power structures and how social change may occur, not only top-down, but also bottom-up. Social scientists have proposed (in addition to such macro-level categories as class or gender) more nuanced and dynamic concepts, such as habitus (Bourdieu, 1972/1977), life experience (Ricoeur, 1984/1988) and lifeworld (Habermas, 1981/ 1987), which mediate between social power structures and individual agents. This guidebook provides help in designing more close-to-life programmes aimed at shaping how people arrange and make sense of their lives and social relations in such areas as contested consumption, risk-taking, health-related activities and other everyday habits that affect well-being. Thus we use the term 'lifestyle' in a broad sense that includes not only individual activities, but also social relations.

Social scientific debate about the possibilities of designing and regulating lifestyles in late modern societies, however, raises the issue of how much legitimacy the state (and authorities in general) has in the private lives of citizens

---

1   'Social structure' is defined as patterns of relationships in society that are arranged by institutions (e.g., political parties) or by cultural norms (e.g., good practices of political campaigns). The meaning of 'social structure' is elaborated on in Chapter 2, section 2.1.

and consumers. The Finnish sociologist Pekka Sulkunen (2010) has presented a convincing argument about the movement from *pastoral* (the paternalistic state as a 'shepherd') to *epistolary* power (guidance from a distance involving 'the ethic of not taking a stand'), resulting in the 'predicament of prevention' (p. 141–2). It is unacceptable in late modern Western societies that a state directly issues orders to people on how to live. Thus the state can, in most cases, only admonish, and arrange a regulatory framework of rules and laws. The latter involves a complex and extensive process of engagement by interested parties, in which severe conflicts of interest surface.

Thus, in this guidebook we address both theoretical and practical conundrums faced by state organisations, civil society organisations[2] and enterprises when they try to regulate and improve (and sometimes police) the whole society's well-being. In late modern societies, there are limits to what kinds of social change programmes can be undertaken. These limits stem not only from the tight purse-strings of organisations and insufficient human resources, but also from political and moral considerations, as the brief argumentation above illustrates. Programme designers need to be informed about these concepts and debates, knowing that all their steps are political: 'life political', to use Giddens's (1991) term.

However, we are conscious of the sometimes frustrating nature of such debates. They may lead to dismay: what can we do, is there a point in any kind of intervention if the state has no legitimacy to intrude into lifestyles and if individuals alone are too enmeshed in their daily habits, and how can difficult social problems be solved at all? This guidebook does not recommend sitting back and doing nothing but theorising. Programmes informed by social theory, close analysis and participation by various stakeholders are, in our view, ways to deal with problems.

Think and stretch

Recall a recent programme or campaign initiated by (a) public or non-profit organisation(s) that has caused controversy in the media.
What was the programme about?
What did the media debate touch upon, and why was the campaign contentious?

There are several ways to shape – directly or indirectly – the ways people lead their lives:

1. an individual recognises a problem and solves it herself (e.g., a young woman quits smoking after getting pregnant, because she knows that smoking is dangerous not only to herself but also to her baby);

---

2 In this book, we use the terms 'civil society organisations' (CSOs) and 'non-governmental organisations' (NGOs) as synonyms.

2. a collective solution is found (e.g., support networks for addicts and individuals suffering from eating disorders);
3. a change is brought about by social pressure (e.g., condemnation of public urination);
4. restrictions are imposed on harmful behaviour (e.g., limits on alcohol sales);
5. useful activities are promoted by changing the physical or virtual environment (e.g., increasing the number of reverse vending machines and collection points for waste paper and dangerous waste).

Figure 1.1   Possible tools of intervention to achieve social change

In the process of seeking solutions, we can distinguish between symbols and material stimuli, between manipulation of the body and of the mind, between voluntary and imposed change, and between people's own initiatives and external institutional intervention. Programme implementers can employ multiple methods and tools, both tangible, such as physical intervention through forming or adjusting the environment and regulations, and intangible, by the use of words, images and sounds (see Figure 1.1).

It is relatively easy to introduce new fads and fashions, but transforming the ways people make sense of and manage their everyday lives is an arduous task, because it involves hundreds of details. The ideal social change programme stimulates processes of *self-regulation* in social groups or the whole society, cultivating the desired behaviour pattern, which reproduces itself so that target audiences accept the recommended practices and apply them in their everyday routines without the need for constant external pressure. This is usually a long process and cannot be achieved with one programme. For example, in Finland the number of fatal fire casualties decreased after smoke detectors were made compulsory, but started to increase again after two years, because detectors' batteries started to die (V. Murd, personal communication, October 8, 2009). Therefore, people were reminded that they needed to check and re-charge them. It is possible that battery inspection will become routine and reminders will become unnecessary. Or household appliances could have a device that prevented them from being switched on before smoke detectors had been checked. Different mechanisms of how social change can be initiated are described in the subsequent section.

Think and stretch

Think about the programmes and projects you have been active in during the past two years. What tools shown in Figure 1.1. have you used? Why? Which ones have you not used? Why not?

1.2 Actors in the field

Changes in individual conduct may be achieved by the efforts of different actors: public administrations, governments, business organisations and civic movements, as well as small changes brought about through individual civic or consumption choices. In practice, the actors of different domains use different means of intervention. Their choices depend on their power and resources, but also on general unwritten codes of conduct. Bourdieu (1972/1977) has described these codes as fields which dictate what kind of strategies and rules should be followed to preserve or gain positions of power in the fields. What is appropriate in the public sector is not appropriate for businesses, and what is allowed in business is not acceptable in civic movements. The programme initiator needs to acknowledge the rules of the game (see Bourdieu in Chapter 2, section 2.1);

the partners from governmental, business and non-governmental sectors need to follow them. Knowledge of the rules of conduct is just as important as knowledge of the behaviour of the final target group of the programme: in order to change someone's conduct, the initiator needs to carefully consider his own.

Public authorities are considered the most powerful actors in addressing social change, because they control tax revenues and exercise legislative and executive power. But life politics is also a part of the agenda of other institutions. Although market mechanisms are often seen as producing social risks and problems, business organisations also increasingly participate in solving social problems, as a part of their social responsibility and marketing initiatives. They offer material resources and know-how to the public and non-profit sectors. Non-governmental organisations, social enterprises and local community groups are often closest to target groups and have ample hands-on knowledge in working with the beneficiaries of the programmes. Expressing their opinions may also bring about new policy interventions.

The connection between the initiatives of different actors is dynamic and complex. For example, various seminal works (e.g., *Risk Society* by the German sociologist Ulrich Beck, 1992) claim that the development of social risks and the *bads* that are produced as side-effects of economic *goods* is always a step ahead of policy interventions. The shortcomings of policy become, in turn, the subjects of social debates and movements.

Tobacco policy is most often referred to as an example of how legislative forces are always a step or two behind market development. The social perception of tobacco problems shifted to health quite recently, when scientific organisations joined the coalition against tobacco. In the US, cigarette television advertising was banned in the 1970s, but when the ads moved to the press it took more than a decade until print advertisements were eliminated. Then in the 1990s the short-term and 'soft' damages caused by smoking were publicised: bad breath, yellow teeth, pimples and poor sports results. Graver health problems were not touched upon (Kluger, 1996/1997). At present people are used to visual warnings on tobacco packaging, which remind them of the harmful effects of smoking. In addition, temporal and spatial restrictions on the sale of alcohol and tobacco products were instituted. In Australia, cigarettes must be sold in standardised brown packs, without any graphic brand elements, only the brand name in standard font. The brown packs are covered with visual and verbal health warnings (see Figure 1.2). The European Union's new tobacco policy (Directive 2014/40/EU, 2014) has been countered by new market innovations: electronic cigarettes, Internet sales of tobacco products etc.

The tobacco industry and trade organisations try to hinder the enactment of regulations by using political channels (lobbying) and media advocacy, and inventing new ways to normalise practices of tobacco use. More about the disputes between government and business organisations can be found in Chapter 4, section 4.2.3. and Chapter 5, section 5.2. Consumption of new tobacco products has developed in parallel with public condemnation and civic drives against tobacco.

Despite the seeming power of public administration, its hands are tied by the bureaucracy of public programmes and rigidly prescribed ways of monitoring target groups' actions. As the use of public money is usually strategically planned to fall between political elections, it is not easy to change the way social problems are dealt with. Public officials often face disputes over how public money should

Figure 1.2   Example of visual warnings on cigarette packages. Plain packages are used in Australia and are planned for launch in France. Visual warnings on cigarette packs are used in many countries worldwide

Photo by Jack Greenmaven via Wikimedia Commons.

be spent. Not only public expectations, but also views of political parties compete. For example, conservative political leaders may be guided by moral beliefs in terms of how social problems should be addressed in public communication. The public sector is also constrained by standardisation. Due to the obligation to treat citizens equally within specific situations, their ability to address individuals whose needs do not fit into pre-determined administrative categories is limited. For example, supporting local employers may be more constructive than paying benefits directly to the unemployed. However, this approach is difficult from the point of view of equal treatment of employers.

The social change programme initiator who wants to co-operate with public sector authorities needs to come to terms with the inconsistencies between historical taken-for-granted procedures and future action, between fluid creativity and strict financial limits, between direct expression of opinions and juggling bureaucratic buzzwords, between real problems and distorted political objectives, between the desires of strong sympathisers and complex hierarchical structures, and between programme visions and the need to report.

The market sector is often underestimated in terms of its impacts on social solutions. However, without material or virtual commodities, the solving of social problems would hardly be possible. Often disappointment in social services may lead to civic initiatives by business enterprises. The tradition of private nursing homes is an example. A saturated market of products and services forces business enterprises to rethink their goals in order to offer services that meet people's needs better or find cause-related roles for themselves in order to justify their presence in the world.

Involving business solutions in a programme, however, may pose several risks. Limitations on finding creative solutions may be financial. In order to invest, business organisations have to negotiate with investors and shareholders, as public administration has to with political party leaders. Therefore, it is natural that businesses have to combine their social objectives with their corporate identities, marketing, brand awareness and cost-effectiveness. It is also common that business leaders believe in market self-regulation (what sells is rational), as it is the core of economic modelling. However, the supply-demand rationality is hard to apply to social problems. The person who is being urged to change his conduct may not be interested in 'buying' the solution (i.e., spending extra money, time or energy). Corporate participation in social change may often face scepticism about its motives: suspicions that behind altruism may lie indirect attempts to increase sales or brand awareness.

As entrepreneurs work on achieving their own goals, the efforts of social activists are focused on influencing problematic businesses, lobbying governmental institutions, and warning the public about social hot spots. For example, the small independent professional team of Avaaz, supported by well-developed technology, is working under heavy time pressure to gather support for geographically and culturally dispersed audiences (http://avaaz.org).

Citizens often step in when the public sector is not able to conform or the market finds a potential reaction unprofitable. Unlike the ready-made products offered by businesses and the top-down guidelines and restrictions imposed by administrative institutions, citizens' initiatives attempt to improve the world from the bottom up, through participatory practices. However, there have been many public accusations that the relationships between governmental and civic organisations

Figure 1.3   People's Climate March in Berlin on 21 September 2014. Avaaz was a prominent organiser (among 1,500 others in the coalition) of the global demonstration against climate change
Photo by Molgreen via Wikimedia Commons.

have become clientelistic, that civic movements are bureaucratised and follow neo-liberal management practices (Choudry and Shragge, 2011; Kohler-Koch and Quittkat, 2013; Martinez, 2009). Therefore, claims that local community-level solutions are more sustainable, because they adapt themselves over time according to the experience of situational needs, should be treated critically.

Present-day associations are less open and attract fewer people than popular movements of the past; they are more specialised and diverse and therefore less visible (Hilton et al., 2010; Putnam, 2000). The ways in which social movements offer a voice to their sympathisers have become more uniform, e.g., simple and short-term contributions, such as donating to a cause or signing a petition.

Think and stretch

Have you ever signed a petition? Do you know how it has affected the targeted problem or what happened afterwards?

However, the ability to act on new social opportunities certainly depends on civic initiatives. For example, in early twentieth-century Bologna, garden plots were associated with the working class, but after World War II working in a garden also became a popular recreational activity among other social groups. Although in many places economic crises have made these gardens sources of food, city dwellers generally associate gardening with cultural, social and civic engagements (Bartoletti, 2013). Sometimes, locally born ideas can also become transferable. Today many cities have provided their inhabitants with plots of land where people can grow their own food: 'green community gardens'.

Think and stretch

Your task is to create and sustain an urban community garden on an available plot of land. What are the first three steps you will take: a) as a municipal official? b) as a community activist?

Citizen initiatives have their advantages and shortcomings. A bottom-up activity usually arises out of a social demand, e.g., for organic garden plots, and not just because it's a 'nice idea'. 'Horizontal' projects provide more room for manoeuvring: people know in broad terms what they want and a better solution emerges naturally through dialogue and practical experience. Endeavours can be too exhausting for the public when officials are appointed to prepare regulations and offer services, sign agreements with citizens and, finally, provide oversight. However, bottom-up initiatives are inefficient when they require implementation and maintenance of vast material resources (such as waste collection infrastructure, from bins to recycling plants), a high degree of standardisation, piles of administrative tasks and stable partnership networks.

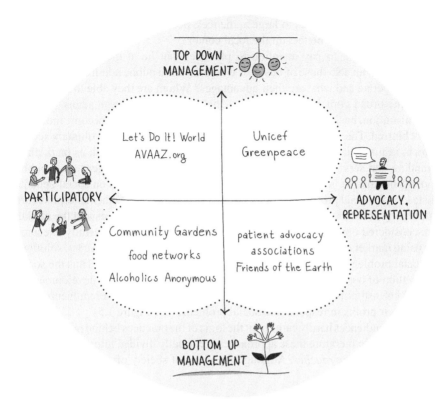

Figure 1.4   Approaches to social change in civic engagement

As in the case of public and business sector representatives, there are particular patterns of conduct in civic society organisations. A potential partner of a voluntary sector activist may find it frustrating that the activist's position fluctuates between zeal and pessimism. Opposition to politics is a source for self-motivation and forms the core of social movements (Habermas, 1981). Criticism of the neo-liberal world order, bohemian appearance, sub-cultural consumption patterns, guerilla tactics, unpaid working hours and discontent with the *vox populi* may well be interwoven with a business-like approach to action.

Civic initiatives cannot be treated uniformly as potential partners or target groups. There are many models of how to differentiate between civic organisations and their operations. We can distinguish between groups that are *orientated to internal relationships (reciprocal activity)*, e.g., such self-help services as Alcoholics Anonymous and food networks, and groups that are orientated to *advocacy* or *influencing the target audience (outward activity)*, e.g., animal protection activists. It is also important to consider management style, whether it is *top-down* or *bottom-up*. While top-down initiatives promise widely understood

targets and effective tactics to large audiences, bottom-up initiatives are believed
to offer solutions that better suit the local context.

It is important to pay attention to practices that lie at the core of citizens'
associations, but also those of business enterprises and public administration. How
do they operate and what are their advantages? Whom are they able to address?

In the broad domain of life politics, the differences between actors – public
administration, businesses and civic society organisations – have become more and
more blurred. The public sector delegates some of its duties to the voluntary sector,
which, in turn, flirts with the practices of the business sector (such as marketing,
branding and services for sale). The business sector is more eager to use public
money, but also to invest in community relations or even focus on social benefits
instead of financial profits. It may be difficult to understand whether enterprises are
addressing consumers' needs or citizens' rights. Although policies and the market
are considered opposing forces, several policies have been successfully executed
by using market mechanisms. An example is social impact bonds (SIBs): solutions
to social problems that the government 'buys' from entrepreneurs. Thus the social
innovation of businesses is transformed into a public service. The development of
beneficial institutional arrangements is also a goal for social entrepreneurs, who
invest their profits in responses to social problems (see Figure 1.5).

Target audiences hardly care about the logic of the practices behind programmes,
but in scientific literature these approaches are usually divided into *consumer-* and
citizen-oriented approaches. Although members of society often play these roles

Figure 1.5   Actors in the field of social change

simultaneously, the roles are contrasted with each other in social theories, media discussions and everyday language (Trentmann, 2007).

Think and stretch
Find out whether there is a law on consumer protection in your country. Which basic rights of consumers are stipulated by that law?

The notion of the *citizen* is related to a society and a community, collective and public interests, responsibility and active participation in society. A citizen is a political subject whose fundamental rights, obligations and freedoms are usually laid down in the constitution. A simple characterisation that is deeply rooted in everyday language and mentality associates *consumers* with private life, desires and needs that are often trivial and can be satisfied by financial deals, indulgence and passiveness. Many social theorists (e.g., Theodor Adorno, Jean Baudrillard, Zygmunt Bauman and Max Horkheimer) have argued that the consumer society is undermining the sense of responsibility, involvement and political zeal of citizens.

Many contemporary theorists, however, have realised that the roles of consumer and citizen are intertwined in everyday life (see e.g., Beck's (1992) treatment of the risk society). Consumption has acquired a political dimension, which is particularly evident in regard to environmentally aware consumption and fair trade. In the English-speaking world, the notion of *citizen-consumer* has been adopted in government policy, uniting the motives and interests of these contrasting roles (see Livingstone, Lunt and Miller, 2007; Spaargaren and Oosterveer, 2010) and stressing that even mundane actions, such as shopping for groceries, have political and globally influential dimensions. At the same time, many interventions are directed at people who are assumed to be responsible, active and aware of, besides personal benefits (e.g., improved health after quitting smoking), the social and even global dimensions of their actions (e.g., using renewable energy).

Dealing with the opposition between the conscientious and active citizen and the passive, hedonistic consumer is not unusual when addressing change from a social practice-based viewpoint, the central conceptual pillar of this book, as its focus is on how a change recruits practitioners both as consumers (users and customers) and citizens (inhabitants and members of a community) (see Figure 1.5). On the mundane consumption level, practitioners cope with change competently, being proud of their everyday achievements (e.g., the transition to a new producer in the energy market), yet at the ideological level they may be disappointed and disengaged from economic and political projects of the elite (such as the liberalisation of the energy market). The ethos of this book focuses on the notions of *engagement* and *empowerment* of practitioners in their complex and entangled roles as citizen-consumers. In the process of planning social change, the most important question that should be addressed is: *how can the envisaged programme engage people so that they become active designers of change to enhance their quality of life?* If this question is the thread running through all stages of project planning and implementation, there is a greater chance of adhering to the values of human well-being and dignity.

Think and stretch

A grocery has opened in Kreutzberg, Berlin[3] that sells unpackaged goods. Imagine that a similar shop has opened near your home. You have to carry your own containers and packaging to the shop. How do you feel about this shop as a citizen? Would you shop there regularly? What pros and cons do you see as a consumer?

At the most general level of programme design, it may be helpful to check both legislation that pertains to citizen and consumer rights and obligations. Even if this legislation is not directly relevant to the programme, it offers a general framework and a guiding light. For example, the citizens of the European Union have many rights within the EU: as passengers, employers, patients etc. The rights of citizens as consumers are protected in the fields of product safety, product performance, e-shopping and equal treatment of residents of different countries. Of course, the programme maker is bound to notice that not all rights and obligations are complied with on a daily basis. Sometimes a separate programme is needed to tackle lacunae or breaches (e.g., if salespeople are reluctant to help consumers exercise their two-year post purchase right of complaint about a faulty good, a programme may be needed both to get consumers to really speak up and to urge shops to accept and deal with complaints without making the consumer feel guilty).

Next, we will introduce some conceptualisations of how the different actors described above can catalyse social change.

1.3 Different approaches to social change

One of the dominant approaches of galvanising lifestyle-related social change is social marketing, with several subdivisions, and a provocative newcomer called 'nudge'. Over the last two decades, a component of soft policy in the public sector that has become increasingly popular is *social marketing*. This concept as an independent domain was introduced in 1969 when Philip Kotler and Sidney Levy suggested (stirring strong passions by doing so) that marketers had been too narrow in their understanding of the field: ' ... marketing is a pervasive societal activity that goes considerably beyond the selling of toothpaste, soap, and steel ... [An] increasing amount of society's work is being performed by organizations other than business firms ... [and] every organization performs marketing-like activities whether or not they are recognized as such' (p. 10).[4] Social marketing

---

3　See http://original-unverpackt.de

4　This statement led to many debates about the market and marketing. We will not deal with those debates in detail; we recommend a relevant overview by Alan Andreasen (2003).

treats people as consumers of potential ideas and (behaviour) recommendations. The development of social marketing has been strongly affected by the theoretical concepts and understandings on which marketing as a research field and a practical activity is based, on highlighting principles of (useful) exchange transactions and rationality.

The concept of *useful transactions* has two branches, which crystallised in the 1970s–80s: the somewhat older 'stream' relies on the use of the commercial sector, distribution, pricing and the branding/advertising of tangible products by the private sector (with the help of governmental subsidies) (Harvey, 1999). For example, in order to control the birth rate in India, condoms and pills have been sold through private-sector companies or by aid agencies at a subsidised price since 1968. These products are branded and marketed with attractive names and packages (references to the Kama Sutra etc.) and assured distribution channels. Statistics shows that consumption of the commercially sold products rose when free dissemination decreased (Madhavan, 2000). Local officials are satisfied with the almost totally commercial approach, because they have found that free items previously handed out in the medical system were often wasted or unused (op. cit.).

The other stream focuses on the government sector and NGOs, which – in close co-operation with advertising agencies – work to design the 'right' messages and communicate them by diverse mass media channels (Manoff, 1985).

The assumption that social change is triggered by the expectation of personal and social gain is clearly expressed in the definition of social marketing provided by Alan Andreasen (1995), an eminent author in the field: 'Social marketing is the application of commercial marketing technologies to the analysis, planning, execution, and evaluation of programs designed to influence the voluntary behaviour of target audiences in order to improve their personal welfare and that of the society of which they are a part' (p. 7). Andreasen agrees with Kotler that people can be made to see the benefits of changed behaviour and persuaded to correct their behaviour. Andreasen's approach and a majority of approaches to marketing are based on the socio-psychological tradition in which the *individual* is highlighted.

Social marketing programmes – similarly to business marketing – make use of a comprehensive marketing mix: product, price, distribution (place) and promotion (Weinreich, n.d.). An individual is seen as an active agent, a consumer, who is offered incentives and benefits for efforts to change behaviour, and for whom barriers are removed to make the desired actions more convenient and recognised. Such marketing focuses on a 'product', which is most often not a physical item, but a clear-cut and relatively simple recommendation, such as 'Eat five portions of fruit and vegetables every day'. Various marketing methods are employed to render the exchange transaction as smooth as possible for the consumer. Here, social marketing is understood as a *technology for changing people's behaviour* (see also Andreasen, 2003).

Recently the individual-focused social marketing thinking has been complemented by an approach aimed at *market change*, which claims that social marketing should focus on the market, as the environment in which everyday transactions are made. Craig Lefebvre (2013), its passionate proponent, argues against the assumption of the individual behaviour change approach of market exchanges as internal rational decision making, and suggests not concentrating on individual behaviour change but on the larger *marketing systems* that cultivate lifestyles and affect society (i.e., by producing social problems as side-effects of their functions). Lefebvre (2013) sees a marketing system as 'people who share a social network and who receive value from each other through meeting or anticipating each other's needs through the exchange of products, services, experiences, and ideas' (p. 64). He gives the example of a health information marketplace, where three types of actors operate: producers of health information (science-based and folklore-based information), mediators of the produced information (marketers of health products) and consumers of that information, who respond by picking up brochures, buying products or treatment regimens, and donating to organisations (Lefebvre, 2013). Lefebvre describes market failures that need to be addressed by social marketing initiatives: imperfect competition (only a few producing or mediating actors), information asymmetry (one actor has better information than other actors) and opportunity costs (alternatives that are not chosen by consumers). These failures need to be addressed by social marketing initiatives (Lefebvre, 2013). Social change initiators must provide people with access to better products and services: ' … social marketing needs to focus on markets and marketplaces. And it needs to focus on the role it plays in helping people access better information, healthier products, better services. That takes us into policy – policy that changes the marketplace and not individual behaviours' (Schwartz, 2010, p. 153). Lefebvre's account is built on the belief in the universality of the private sector's business model and the marketing principle as a systematic way to solve the core business problem of achieving *organised success* by satisfying consumers' everyday wants and needs. Thus a simple transfer is made by him to the field of social problems.

Think and stretch

Have you encountered a situation where a product or service helps people to change their behaviour?

Another widespread stream of thought is behavioural economics, with its popular offspring: the psychology-based 'choice architecture' proposed by the economist Richard Thaler and the legal scholar Cass Sunstein (2008) in their well-known book *Nudge*. They advocate a libertarian paternalism in which policies, environments and regulations should nudge individuals to make better choices. This approach has been warmly welcomed by the governments of the US, the UK and Australia. In the US, the 'nudge' approach has been relied on to work out a new pension scheme, and in the UK to improve compliance in tax reporting and to lower alcohol consumption among youth. Overall, however, 'nudging' in public policy-making has had varied levels of success (Hansen and Jespersen, 2013).

The authors' theoretical arguments stem from public policy principles and applied behavioural sciences. Their core belief is that public policy relies too much on people's deliberate choices and decision-making capabilities, whereas it is cheaper and communicatively less problematic to employ human automatic behaviour by creating systems of default selections (like default settings on our computers). Policy makers may like this idea because it is less costly, avoiding legal injunctions and incentives. Also they avoid being blamed for restricting freedom of choice (as the individual may opt out of a default). However, nudge-thinking has raised both ethical and political concerns (e.g., Evans, 2012; Mettler, 2011), as well as practical scepticism (e.g., Farrell and Shalizi, 2011). For example, Thaler and Sunstein (2008) urged people to donate their body organs if they died unexpectedly, by making organ donation an opt-out rather than an opt-in choice. However, there is a lack of evidence that the opt-out schemes actually increase donations (Healy, 2006).

Such arguments are vehemently debated (see e.g., Hansen and Jespersen, 2013), but our main attention is on the practical aspects. The claim that human decision making is not perfectly rational, as the traditional economic models assume, corresponds well with the social practice-based approach advocated in this book. Proceeding from this, Thaler and Sunstein (2008) focus on how to change the decision-making context. A simple example is displaying healthy food at eye-level, with high-sugar, high-fat foods at lower or higher levels. This solution intervenes in retailers' food arrangements in order to 'nudge' consumers and might prove difficult to negotiate with shops.

In addition, Thaler and Sunstein offered to increase people's pension savings by creating automatic enrolment in a certain pension programme if no action were taken; they claimed that this would increase the profits of insurance companies. Thus the connections between the governmental sector and private business are reinforced by experts who design 'nudge' ideas. Studies of such experiments have been established in the UK and elsewhere. 'Nudging' does not rule out legal regulation of private businesses or, in some cases, NGOs (bans and injunctions may be needed to implement the 'nudges'), but not needing to provide information to citizens (which is one of the cornerstones of social marketing) can lead to considerable savings. Yet the question looms large: if the government decides to introduce some kind of default option, should the citizens be informed about it? For example, if someone plans to renew her driver's license, should she be informed and prepared emotionally to make the decision about whether or not she would like to be an organ donor? Many private businesses operate on default choices, which has induced consumer protection authorities to call for more explicit information to clients (e.g., in the financial services sector), and has led to awareness raising and protest campaigns by civic activists. If the same actions are induced by governmental nudging, savings from communication become of questionable value.

Figure 1.6 A TV crew from National Geographic tested whether collisions in Washington, D.C. involving gaming and texting pedestrians could be avoided by regulating the use of public side-walks. This experiment was done in the crowded city of Chongqing, China.

The authors of this book agree with the 'nudge' critics who point out arguments in support of democracy. What are democratic and civic ways to give feedback to the designers of choice architecture? Farrell and Shalizi (2011, para. 6) have claimed that choice architecture 'offers no means for ordinary people to comment on, let alone correct, the technocrats' prescriptions. This leaves technocrats with no systematic way of detecting their own errors, correcting them, or learning from them. And technocracy is bound to blunder, especially when it is not democratically accountable'.

In order to offer innovative yet acceptable ideas for 'nudges', co-creation (crowd-sourcing) rather than solo efforts by (economic or technical) experts are more fruitful, from the point of view of democracy as well as of creativity. The 'diversity trumps ability' theory of Scott E. Page (2007) states that groups of agents with diverse understandings of the world solve difficult problems better than narrowly focused groups with higher expertise.

Think and stretch
Look at Figure 1.6. Imagine that similar street marking was done on the most crowded pedestrian street of your home town. What would be the implications?

In summary, choice architecture, or 'nudge', if put into operation in full swing may not be as simple, cost-saving or effective as it might seem in an experimental setting. There are still costs for information campaigns (the default setting cannot be done covertly in democratic societies due to real political opposition, consumer protection organisations and free media). Default settings may arouse protest and resistance from consumers, private enterprises and NGOs when their business interests or ideals are threatened by regulations. Whenever intelligent citizen-consumers are involved, discussion may surface and that automatically adds complexity. Thus the beauty of the cost savings and technical simplicity of some of the 'architectured choices' are eroded, as is their novelty compared to 'traditional' social marketing.

Conceptually both 'nudgers' and social marketers treat individuals and their choices as the roots of social change. This inevitably focuses analysis and the location of desired and designed change on the individual mind. In addition, both camps' proponents tend to see policy makers and policies as outsiders in the problems they are trying to solve. This guidebook positions policies and programmes within the dynamics of social change and seeks holistic solutions that address consumer-citizens who are engaged, and often entangled in, various interwoven social practices that cannot be altered by individual choice alone. For example, studies on green practices indicate that, besides creating infrastructure (e.g., a public transport network), attention to community norms is also important (Kahn and Morris, 2009) and, therefore, programmes seeking social change should adopt a comprehensive approach to the social environment and the people who lead their everyday lives within that environment.

1.4 Summary

Life politics means that social problems and social change are not only about the large macro-level issues of tackling poverty and social inclusion, but also about the 'meso'-level lifestyle-related problems of eating, drinking, spending money or waste sorting, which in aggregate become political questions of national health, sustainability and security. Seemingly light-weight themes often invite solutions such as awareness campaigns and other individual-oriented efforts to educate and persuade people to be more responsible. This might be justified in some cases, yet, as research indicates, such campaigns are often of questionable value in terms of actually changing people's behaviour. Using only intangible methods and means – informing, encouraging and coaxing – which are at first glance easily accessible and less resource consuming than changing infrastructure or product innovation, is limited, in terms of breadth and power, when it comes to transforming people's everyday lives. Creating a new normality is a complex process of practice change.

Although 'lifestyle' is usually associated with consumption and markets, our point of departure is that roles and practices of consumers and citizens are intertwined. In order to shape the practices of consumer-citizens meaningfully – engaging the latter in co-creation – it is not useful to merely sprinkle correct answers in citizens' paths so that they can automatically adopt them as default choices; different players in the field should avoid being defensive about their own jurisdiction and areas of responsibility, and develop a holistic approach in which the practices at the root of the social problems are taken as starting points. Each different field (policy or market) has its own rules of the game. Therefore establishing co-operation, or at least some liaison, between different domains and interests, and avoiding turf wars, is a hard nut to crack, yet there is no other option. This is the case when social practices that strive to make people do some things in their lives differently, whether being more sustainable, financially literate, responsible or healthier, are taken seriously. More flesh will be added to these bones in the following chapters.

Further Reading

Textbooks, manuals and practical online resources

European Commission (2014, September 2). Eco-innovation. When business meets the environment. Retrieved from http://ec.europa.eu/environment/eco-innovation/

Kotler, P. and Lee, N. (2008). *Social marketing: Influencing behaviours for good* (3rd ed.). Los Angeles, CA: Sage.

Lefebvre, C.R. (2013). *Social marketing and social change: Strategies and tools for improving health, well-being, and the environment.* San Francisco, CA: Jossey-Bass.

Thaler, R.H., and Sunstein, C.R. (2008). *Nudge. Improving decisions about health, wealth, and happiness.* New Haven, CT: Yale University Press.

The Young Foundation (n.d.). Webpage introducing the Young Foundation. Retrieved from http://youngfoundation.org/

Weinreich, N.K. (n.d.). What is social marketing? Retrieved from http://www.social-marketing.com/Whatis.html

Theoretical approaches and publications based on empirical research

Fisher, W.F. (1997). Doing good? The politics and antipolitics of NGO practices. *Annual Review of Anthropology* 26, 439–64. doi:10.1146/annurev.anthro.26.1.439

Livingstone, S., Lunt, S. and Miller, L. (2007). Citizens, consumers and the citizen-consumer: Articulating the citizen interest in media and communications regulation. *Discourse and Communication* 1, 63–89. doi:10.1177/17504813 07071985

Schwartz, B. (2010). An interview with Craig Lefebvre. *Social Marketing Quarterly* 16, 151–4. doi:10.1080/15245004.2010.526849

Shove, E. and Spurling, N. (eds). (2013). *Sustainable practices: Social theory and climate change.* London, England: Routledge.

Spaargaren, G. and Oosterveer, P. (2010). Citizen-consumers as agents of change in globalizing modernity: The case of sustainable consumption. *Sustainability* 2, 1887–1908. doi:10.3390/su2071887

Warde, A. and Southerton, D. (eds) (2012a). *The habits of consumption.* Helsinki, Finland: Helsinki Collegium for Advanced Studies.

Reports and policy documents

Department for Children, Schools and Families, Department for Culture, Media and Sport. (2009). The impact of the commercial world on children's wellbeing. Report of an independent assessment. Retrieved from https://www.education.gov.uk/publications/eOrderingDownload/00669-2009DOM-EN.pdf

Chapter 2
Social practices as sites of social change

This chapter gives the programme maker a theoretical framework and some tools for argumentation to reconcile various partners' and stakeholders' conceptual dissent on different strategies. To do that, Anthony Giddens's take on the sociological debate on agency and structure is put in context, and practice-based and individual behaviour-change approaches are compared. Next, the chapter divides social practices into interacting elements that are relatively easy to fathom. These provide a foundation for subsequent programme preparation and implementation.

This chapter juxtaposes the practice-based approach of the present handbook with competing ones that all aim to change people's behaviour. Understanding theoretical premises helps to reconcile differences in opinions that project partners and stakeholders may have about the effectiveness of the strategies of change.

A social practice is a *nexus of doings and sayings* (Schatzki, 2002), a recognisable pattern of action that is a basic unit of social processes. We briefly review social theories that have inspired the practice-change approach. Then we explain how the latter differs from individual behaviour change. Finally, the dynamics and elements of social change are examined at a micro level, preparing the foundation for designing a sociologically informed change programme.

2.1 Agency and structure as the inspiration for practice theories

This section discusses a central question in social theory: which are more central in changing individuals' actions: 1) individuals' autonomous choices or 2) recurring patterns of social constraints and opportunities?

To resolve the conflict between individual will and social determinacy, several social theories have been developed, for example by Anthony Giddens, his main critic Margaret Archer and Pierre Bourdieu. They discuss voluntarism and determinism, which question the power balances between individuals and social structure in defining truth, as well as subjectivism and objectivism, which question the nature of truth. To exemplify these -isms, several attempts to change individual action are displayed in Figure 2.1.

As presented here, policy mechanisms and resulting (communication) campaigns emanate from an objectivist belief that reality exists independent of individuals' opinions about it. Reality can be measured by scientific methods, although only approximately and with errors. The goal of the campaigner is to

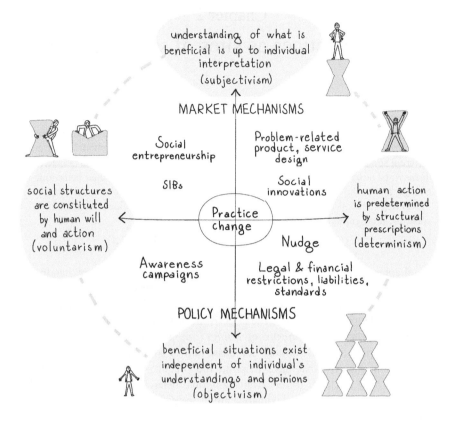

Figure 2.1   Different approaches to social change

show reality to the individual. By doing so, campaigners are also voluntarist: they assume that if future risks are presented to individuals, they will take action in order to eliminate risks (avoiding problems through rational thinking). These premises are very common in the behaviour-change approach.

Nudge followers and social impact bond proponents pursue a more determinist approach. They assume that individuals' actions are shaped by structural preconditions. Therefore, they want to change structures. Social impact bond and market-based approaches derive from the belief that individuals' opinions are more accurate in explaining social situations and related needs (subjectivism) than are orthodox scientific descriptions. Indeed, objectivist science has found proof of the shortcomings of 'rational-choice' campaigns, which are enforced by positivist policy mechanisms and have been imitated by civic initiatives. The crisis in such a behaviour-change approach has provoked a search for better strategies of change. Figure 2.1 shows how the practice-based approach (in the middle) shares many common features with other strategies of change.

Figure 2.2   Sir Anthony Giddens talking about climate change in Policy Network 2009 (Policy Network on Flickr, 2009)

The most familiar attempts to unite the ideas of *structure* and *agent* have been made by the British sociologist Anthony Giddens in his book *Constitution of Society* (1984/1989) and the French anthropologist Pierre Bourdieu (in *Outline of a Theory of Practice*, 1972/1977). The treatment of agent-structure dilemmas is remarkably similar by both authors. However, Bourdieu is claimed to have chosen a more objectivist and determinist approach (thinking rationally is just an option for an individual) and Giddens a more subjectivist and essentially voluntarist position (the agent's intention is a means to order social structure) (Archer, 1995; King, 2000; Mouzelis, 2000; Schatzki, 1997).

Researchers who draw on Giddens (1984/1989) and his structuration theory oppose the deep-rooted belief that an individual is a passive participant, a mere recipient of reasonable and correct messages communicated by a system. They argue that an individual is an active agent who shapes the institutions of society – values, social norms, power relations, resources and practices – and society is not a collective reality, but a structure that both constrains and enables the activities of the individual.

By using the phrase *the duality of structure*, Giddens (1984/1989) emphasises that structure is both a medium and an outcome of the reproduction of practices. For example, as public relations practitioners carry out short-term public awareness campaigns in order to change individuals' behaviour, it is not the impact of their efforts, but the campaigning as a practice *per se* that legitimises its continuation.

All this nourishes the belief that change in individuals' behaviour depends on their relevant knowledge, which, in turn, reinforces the use of information campaigning.

Agency, as Giddens (1984/1989) calls it, is the ability of an individual to function within the structure of a society (to observe or create rules, and to use or shape resources). It is the conscious ability of the individual to impact her social reality. Agency should not be treated as the acknowledged conduct of an individual in its ordinary sense (e.g., as a conscious rational decision), because a large number of people's everyday activities are constituted by *routinised habits and skills*, a large part of which involves unacknowledged and embodied skills (such as chopping and peeling to prepare a meal, driving, or using a keyboard: we only become aware of these skills if we are expected to have them but do not). Even if an individual's conduct is intentional, it is always accompanied by the unintentional: e.g., those who carry out public campaigns occupy public discussion and advertising space that cannot be used by others at the same time.

Both for Giddens and Bourdieu, individuals' practices evolve in the course of socialisation, especially in early childhood. However, Giddens (1984/1989) emphasises the importance of physical and social routines (repeated conduct) in the confirmation of the effectiveness and social appropriateness of a specific action. For him, individual action develops in the co-operation between (1) unconscious, repressed motivational elements, (2) *practical consciousness*, which operates in a tacit and often bodily manner, and (3) *discursive consciousness*, which captures the individual's reflective skills. Giddens's view on individual action is social: triggered and shaped in the interaction of individuals. For Bourdieu (1972/1977) the continuation of practice is less social, and more up to practical sense and bodily dispositions that naturalise social order. Bourdieu opposes the view of an individual as a fully rational actor and applies the notion of *habitus*. Habitus is the way external social structures are internalised in human bodily conduct; for example, individuals tend to view their preferences of taste as natural, although class belonging has a great impact. Instead of continuous rational calculation, individuals act according to their understanding of the games people play in society. However, similar to Giddens's practical consciousness, the rules of the game appear to individuals as given (Bourdieu's *doxa:* the congruence of internal and external structures), inducing individuals to go on with the game. But Bourdieu's approach to potential change in individuals' practice is tighter, as it is bound up with the notion of *field*, which dictates the game that the actor is taught to play. Therefore, games are specific to the economic field, cultural field, religious field etc. For most people the existence of rules of the game – formal and written, as well as informal tacit ones – does not constitute a problem. It would be outrageous to mix the rules of football, for example, with rugby. We argue that one of the rules of the behaviour-change game is the 'naturalness' of public awareness campaigns as tools for change. Vast networks of people depend on this: public officials, media and advertising professionals, and educators.

Most awareness raising programmes address discursive consciousness without considering practical consciousness. However, in order to achieve stability, the desired change has to be adopted at the level of practical conduct, and become internalised in bodily dispositions. But when aiming to change these dispositions intentionally, one should be very cautious. According to Giddens (1984/1989), the stability of practical conduct is a prerequisite for maintaining an unconscious sense of security. Even tiny rearrangements in shopping displays, e-banking environments or in domestic kitchens can be very irritating. Large interventions in people's everyday socio-material world may provoke a sense of insecurity and helplessness.

Think and stretch

In the shopping context, Giddens's duality of structure means that everyday consumer choices reproduce the supply and choice of products. Have you also exercised more active forms of re-shaping structure: e.g., have you expressed your preferences in products, or joined any consumer protest campaigns?

For a programme initiator, it is also important to envision the triggers behind social reproduction, as spatial and temporal recurrence of the desired practice is the outcome that a social change programme aims at.

For Giddens (1984/1989), the structural positioning of the use of rules and resources drives social practices. Modifications in rules and resources are not entirely up to individuals or their social reflexivity (which is not a frequent mode of being anyway). Individual reflexivity is typically oriented to the analysis of the outcome of conduct. But human conduct does not result only in intended consequences; it usually causes unintended consequences in other spheres of life. For example, a parent striving for professional development in order to be successful in the labour market may have to work more hours and is, therefore, not able to spend as much time with his children. This, in turn, may have an effect on family life that may eventually put the social structure out of balance. The necessity of replacing the missing person in family relations may provoke a space for new social institutions: nannies, kindergartens, extra social benefits etc. For Giddens (1984/1989), the unintended consequences of action form the motivation for reflexive monitoring of action and, therefore, for social change.

For Bourdieu (1972/1977), the dynamics of social structure are activated by the exchange of capitals that are used in the interplay between different fields. For him, the conversion of capitals – such as economic (money and material resources), cultural (manners, artwork and official recognition), social (social relations, access to networks and trust) and symbolic (reputation in the eyes of relevant stakeholders) – guarantees continuation of rule reproduction in particular fields, as well as the existence of social groups who, in order to exist, need to accumulate particular types of capital.

Although the triggers of the dynamics of social practice are different for Giddens and Bourdieu, their explanations of the order of triggers are both insufficient

(Archer, 2012; King, 2000) and have provoked criticism of their theoretical ideas, as well as inspiring many meso- and micro-level theories.

Think and stretch

Recall a recent public awareness campaign that was related to your lifestyle. Did you change any of your habits? What sort of structural changes (e.g., product selection or regulations) would be needed to make you change your habits?

Grand social theories are useful for the analysis of social change, but they do not answer the question of how to build well-functioning social relations that can be perceived as a 'natural order of things'. The analysis of social structure is complicated and offers endless opportunities. Therefore, it is irresponsible to plan a social change without addressing the complexity the individual is faced with. Our handbook provides guidance on this road.

2.2 Changing social practices or individual behaviour?

Sustainable consumption is useful in exemplifying the application of social practice theory. There is ample research into sustainable consumption and pro-environmental activities showing that individual behaviour-change programmes are ineffective in solving environmental problems (e.g., Oosterveer and Spaargaren 2011; Shove and Spurling, 2013; Warde and Southerton, 2012a). People's everyday lives involve a number of activities that are 'harmful' to the environment (from forms of transport to eating habits). To put it simply, we may say that attempts to make individual behaviour more sustainable presume that if people are sufficiently aware of the potential consequences of their behaviour, their adoption of 'greener' attitudes and pro-environmental behaviour will be a natural outcome. If we observe our own everyday life in detail, we see how complicated it is to transform our patterns of behaviour. Quit showering every day? Stop eating wheat and sugar? Walk to work? Easier said than done. Research has shown that pro-environmental activity is often brought about by a complex network of influences: from the behaviour of a girlfriend to the opening of a new organic shop in the neighbourhood. Rather than leading the way, attitudes may lag behind and, contrary to common belief, they are often outcomes of activities (Bartiaux and Salmón, 2012).

The group of theorists and researchers whom we are primarily inspired by firmly believe that the focus of analysis and the target of social change programmes need to be shifted from individual behaviours to *social practices*. Nicola Spurling, Andrew McMeekin, Elizabeth Shove, Dale Southerton and Daniel Welch (2013) have used the iceberg metaphor: behaviours are only the tip above the water. Social practices as entities, which configure individual action, form the part that lies under the water. This is what needs to be addressed, first making it visible by analysis and then figuring out ways of transformation. In the next sections we outline the basics of social practice-based thinking to provide theoretical guidance to programme designers. Sometimes resorting to theory and research can prove to be useful in defending a programme that might at first seem too unorthodox to decision-makers.

The central claim of social practice researchers is that more sustainable and healthier ways of living are not only a matter of individual choice, but also involve larger socio-cultural, economic and technical transitions that re-define 'normal' social patterns of activity or nexuses of sayings and doings. This approach is far from mainstream. Individualist behaviour-change thinking is deeply rooted, as shown above, in the neo-liberal political doctrine (delegating responsibility to the individual and keeping the role of the state minimal), as well as in economics- and psychology-based popular understandings of human behaviour. Policy documents and social marketing campaign briefs abound in such terms as 'awareness', 'attitudes' and 'behaviour'.

Before going on to the social practice theory, it is useful to examine the behaviour-change world-view in some detail and then introduce the main points of criticism of it. The three central notions are: individual *knowledge, attitudes* and *behaviour*. One of the best-known theories in this context is the *theory of planned behaviour*, proposed by Icek Ajzen (1985) as a development of the theory of reasoned action. Its precepts are the following:

1. the main actor is the *individual*, i.e., the target group of any intervention is the person (not a family or a team of employees, let alone the more abstract category of 'carriers of a specific social practice');
2. the individual is a *maker of rational choices* which are manifested in behavioural intentions;
3. knowledge, attitudes (including perceived behavioural control, i.e., one's belief in the ability to accomplish a planned action) and behaviour are *related* in a linear manner: to put it simply, more knowledge leads to 'righter' attitudes and more self-efficacy, which in turn lead to the desired action.

Many communication and especially marketing textbooks use the following simplified scheme of planning communication: first, the target group has to be *informed* about the desired outcome or object; then *attitudes are shaped* and only after an individual is sufficiently informed and has the 'right' attitude, his or her *behaviour is changed* (as examples of recent textbooks see e.g., Cornelissen, 2008; Wilson and Ogden, 2008). Such accounts draw their inspirations from the so-called AIDA (attention, interest, desire, action) model of advertising originating from the end of the nineteenth century in the USA. Such accounts proceed from the model of 'hierarchy of effects', which was originally designed by Jean Lavidge and Etienne Steiner in 1961 and consists of six elements: awareness, knowledge, liking, preference, conviction and purchase. This model invites campaigners to first set *cognitive objectives* ('what the target audience should know'), then *affective objectives* ('what the target audience should feel and think') and finally *conative objectives* ('what the target audience should do'). Yet this book asks the campaigner – at least temporarily – to leave aside the linearly programmable individual and come along on the following thinking exercise.

We can imagine a landscape where change is desired being embedded in a socio-material network where people, things, environments, documents, technologies and various other meaningful units form interconnected nodes. How to conduct an analysis of this nexus for a particular programme is examined in the next chapter. Within that network, a *territory* can be delineated, i.e., an open-ended area which is feasible to address with a potential programme. Boundary drawing, at this very initial stage, is not so much a science as an art, and thus can be approached creatively based on the expert knowledge of the programme designer (see Figure 2.3).

What if the basic question to ask is not 'what do people know and what do they think and feel?', but 'what do different groups of people do?' What sorts of activities unfold in the territory and what is the territory itself like? In other words, what is the context – the network of interrelations of material, legal, social,

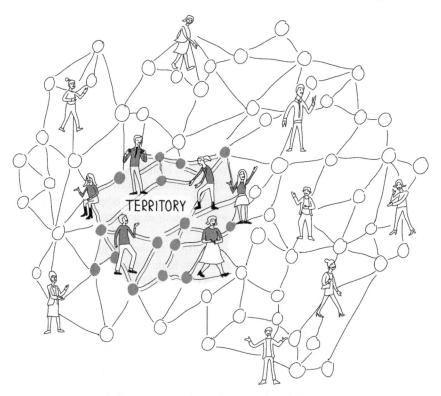

Figure 2.3   Socio-material network connected by nodes and the programme territory

economic and cultural nodes – that shapes the ways people do the particular thing we want to change? For example, if the desired outcome is making people eat more fruit and vegetables, the activities to be considered are not only eating, but also cooking, shopping, perhaps also gardening, having lunch at work and at school, enjoying a family dinner etc. All these activities can be made sense of as social practices.

According to the renowned practice theorist Ted Schatzki (1996), a practice is a network of particular *doings* and *sayings* that is held together and joined into a meaningful entity by certain elements. In other words, a practice is composed of a set of actions that are recognised in a certain social environment as meaningful. For example, think of what a family dinner consists of in your culture. What sorts of material objects are needed? What do people do? What do they need to know and be capable of in order to take part in the dinner properly, and what is considered unacceptable? What are the meanings that lie behind the activity?

It is difficult to differentiate between different practices, and theorists disagree about this aspect. Most practices occur as a bundle and people are likely to be engaged in several of them at the same time: e.g., listening to music and using a keyboard while keeping an eye on a news programme on TV. Also, it is obvious that even if we recognise something as a set of activities belonging to the same practice (lunch in a school canteen, or a university lecture) its manifestations vary across socio-cultural settings, and vary when different practitioners perform them on different occasions. Indeed, this makes the picture quite fuzzy. Yet, we ask for patience on this theoretical journey.

Think and stretch
Look at Figure 2.4. This picture shows an everyday traffic practice in a city. What factors (e.g., urban planning, social norms etc.) affect this problem? What is the space of your individual freedom of choice here?

It has probably become obvious to the reader by now that the theory of social practices (*practice theory*) is not an unequivocal and coherent theoretical framework; it is a set of notions that in the opinion of many authors can explain social change and the possibilities of bringing it about better than the planned behaviour and individual-centred approaches do. To put it simply, practices are located between the social agent and social structure (described in the previous chapter), uniting the two. When we analyse patterns of activity, we need to probe deeply into both the activities of individuals (focusing on patterns of activity, not on the characteristics of individuals) and the structural environment in which those activities occur. How to do this analysis properly is highlighted in the next chapter. In their everyday lives, people engage in performances – of transport, of child rearing, of office work, of cooking, of cleaning and laundering, of entertaining guests etc. – and by doing so they can and do change the existing reality, including the social structure.

Figure 2.4   A traffic flow in Moscow
Photo by Aare Abrams

The thesis that an individual is not a central actor in the social analysis but a carrier of practices may seem somewhat odd, yet it is instructive for the present purposes. If we take a closer look at our own everyday lives, it becomes clear that a number of familiar and habitual activities are carried out semi-automatically, without deliberation (see Giddens's 'practical consciousness' in section 2.1 above). We make coffee every day, yet we do not deliberate over the minutest detail: how to pour the water or push the button. It is a habit. People are immersed in practices, doing things that they are used to doing routinely. In spite of small variations, there are larger patterns of routines and webs of activities that many people in a given socio-cultural and economic context do in a similar manner: social norms of cleanliness make us do laundry several times a week, we need to get to work on time, so it may be more expedient to drive than to walk etc.

Institutional interventions that are concerned with social change and inducing people to, for example, use more public transport or bicycles for commuting are not aimed at changing the individual. Their objective is to produce bigger reconfigurations of normality (otherwise no real reduction in environmental damage is feasible). This is, however, a long and complex process, in which an important role is played by not only rational thinking, attitudes and judgements of the individual but also by many intertwined social phenomena, including the path dependence and inertia of the surrounding material and technological systems (e.g., in order to ensure that waste is sorted, separate containers have to be provided to households and offices; there has to be room for several dustbins in the kitchen, etc.).

From the perspective of interventions, the value of the theoretical framework introduced here is the understanding that to achieve more profound social change, especially pertaining to people's lifestyles, we need a comprehensive approach to social life. An analysis of and focusing on a network of practices (as opposed to individual attitudes) may seem complicated in a situation where 'there is money available and a campaign to organise', but this has the potential to detect the aspects of everyday life that can be changed if they are targeted in a more holistic way. To use a plant metaphor, the social practice approach may help to determine the location, soil and types of plants that have the potential to grow and flourish in a particular garden, i.e., to shape a new normality that lasts.

While not denying that the theories of social practices have their strong points, we do not underestimate the importance of the individual thinking and making decisions (the existence of habit and routines does not mean that there is no rational deliberation). Our aim is not to fall into the normative trap, which looms large if individuals are treated as dupes who act based on habit only and thus can be manipulated by well-meaning policy makers, nudgers and social marketers. A very pure version of practice theory may sometimes separate questions of the attitudes and values of people whose lives are to be reformed, as Andrew Sayer (2013) aptly highlights in his sympathetic critique in a recent book *Sustainable practices: Social theory and climate change*.

However, our premise still is that any attempt to delegate the success of social change solely to the individual, hoping that it can be achieved by targeting his/her knowledge and attitudes, is limited and resource consuming. Also, we consider the 'nudge' approach narrow, because it sets restrictions or latently imposes new duties on the performance of existing practices, but does not reform the practices. Our idea is to encourage practice change that takes root and will be reproduced in the course of socialisation.

Table 2.1　　Individual behaviour and social practice approaches: their basic tenets and differences

Changing individual behaviour	Changing social practices
Basic unit of analysis	
Individual	Social practice as an organised bundle of activities, doings and sayings
Nature of human activity	
Mostly rational, calculated and reflective	Often non-rational, ambivalent, Often semi-automatic, habituated
Linkage between activity components	
Linear (from attitude to behaviour)	No linear connection; possible value action gap
Agent	
Individual	Collective (e.g., the household). Emphasis on social relations and interaction between people (including power relations). Attempt to define relevant parties involved in problematic practices
Drivers of action	
Individual choice, decision	A network of different factors related to practice (relations, material objects, events)
Source of social change	
Individual choices, decisions that change their behaviour	Change of practices as collective social entities (breaking old ties between practice elements and the creation of new ones)
Role of environment (including institutions and infrastructure)	
Environment as a barrier or motivator for desired individual behaviour. External context to behaviour	Environment as integral to practice. Constant co-involvement and interaction of everyday life and institutional and socio-technical environments/systems
Position of policy and other interventions	
An external force that has an impact on factors and drivers of behaviour	No external force; embedded in the systems of practice; policy influenced by the same practices it seeks to influence

Means and instruments	
Mainly texts and symbols: raising awareness, dissemination of knowledge and shaping of attitudes	Focus on bodily and material elements, things and infrastructure (touch-points), as well as regulation. Creation of an environment (both material and symbolic, social) which impedes the spread of undesired practices or favours the desired practices
Transfer of experience and lessons	
Clear universal mechanisms, universal laws. The same question – the same answer regardless of context	Historical, cultural, social specifics of each case. Transfer of experience very limited. New context – new answer to the same question

Author's synthesis from Ajzen (1991), Stern (2000), Shove (2010), Shove et al (2012), Hargreaves (2011) and Evans et al (2012).

Table 2.1 summarises the opposition between the individual behaviour-change approach and practice-based approach. It is important to bear in mind that all programmes are part of social reality and their designers cannot view themselves as parts of the external environment or as syringes that can inject desired change into some insulated terrain. Programmes are always outcomes of and constrained and enabled by previous programmes, histories of organisations, policies and regulations that may be directly or indirectly parts of the problem to be solved. Programmes and problems co-evolve and mutate constantly; they do not exist on different planets.

2.3 Anatomy and types of social practices

Elizabeth Shove and Mika Pantzar (2005) have proposed one of the simplest and most intriguing analyses of the components of practices (see also Shove, Pantzar and Watson, 2012). Shove has also been one of the most influential advocates of social practice theory-based policy making. The following discussion is inspired by the above-mentioned authors' work, yet also 'translates' it into the language of the campaigner and programme designer, in addition to providing hands-on analysis guidance in the next chapter. According to their approach, each practice is comprised of three key components:

Meaning refers to any interpretation that people can attribute to a practice. For example, the meaning of smoking changed significantly over the twentieth century. While in the middle of the century doctors recommended smoking as a means of relaxing, some decades later smoking was clearly interpreted as harmful to health. Moreover, there is the issue of the damaging effect of passive smoking: smoking is officially seen as bad not only for the smoker but also for others, which clearly acts on people's guilt and sense of responsibility as members of society.

**Figure 2.5   A US trade card from the end of the nineteenth century,
featuring Pet brand cigarettes (Boston Public Library, 2013)**

Thus the category of meaning may embrace a wide variety of understandings, images and ideologies. Different groups of practitioners, as well as outsiders, understand a practice differently. For a teenage smoker, the meaning may be about rebellion against the adult world, about bonding and belonging with peers or just about boredom and finding something to kill time. For a middle-aged man who has tried several times to quit smoking without success, it may be both about addiction and not achieving control over his body, as well as about precious moments of peace and relaxation in the midst of a hectic life. A newly pregnant woman may, however, interpret smoking altogether differently: thinking about guilt and the health of the baby.

Think and stretch
Look at this more than a century-old cigarette promotion. How has the meaning of smoking changed in your country?

The second component essential to a practice is comprised of *materials and things*. These are specific objects that are necessary to perform a practice (you need a car to drive or a cigarette to smoke), as well as the material and technical space and infrastructure that make an activity possible (e.g., roads and parking lots, rooms for smokers). It is obvious that practices are certain to change when things and material environments are altered, because the present theoretical view sees environments and things not as external contexts or even barriers to a practice, but as integral parts of it. People need things to engage in a practice. Yet limiting social change to banning or replacing objects or environmental elements may be far too inadequate to tackle a substantial problem. Some of the 'nudges' referred to in Chapter 1, section 1.3 consist of 'default' changes in the material environment. For example, there is the infamous failed plan in New York to prohibit the sale of many sweetened drinks in more than half-litre containers in order to reduce excessive sugar intake. However, the change concerned only one detail in the intricate network of 'obesity practices'. The attempt fell through when the state's highest court ruled after long litigation that the New York City Board of Health had exceeded its regulatory authority. It is difficult to analyse to what extent it is affordable and legitimate for states, local governments or private enterprises to change material environments and infrastructures. However, it is clear that in most cases some material re-design is needed in almost every social change attempt. There are very few things in people's daily lives that are transformable only through cognitive means, i.e., by issuing battle calls or moral admonishing to 'think differently'. This sometimes tends to be forgotten because people trained to create campaigns have a words-and-symbols-oriented mindset, which has roots in the textual and book-based culture and education of the Western world. Yet, it is essential to bear in mind: things matter!

The third component is comprised of the *skills and competence* needed to perform an activity. They are both cognitive and bodily, both discursive/reflective as well as practical/tacit (e.g., after a person learns to ride a bicycle, the skill is preserved in his/her body and cannot be forgotten). The example of driving a car is very illustrative because the skill is regulated in detail through traffic regulations and intricate license acquiring procedures. The aim of national rules is to ensure a level of competence that guarantees the safety of all road users. At the same time, driving is a very physical activity, a large part of which is performed almost automatically, i.e., 'the foot knows when and where to push'. There is no conscious deliberation before each movement: the experience/skill is physical in the direct sense of the word.

Although Shove et al. (2012) do not mention *social interaction* explicitly in their model, the authors of this guidebook are convinced that social practices cannot be comprehensively analysed without social interaction (see also Christensen and Røpke, 2010). Social interaction refers to any relationship between individuals and groups. It includes the interpretation of, and attributing meanings to, the acts of an interaction partner. This includes more than linguistic interaction. We are dealing with 'exchanges' that are both physical and mental. In simplified terms, these exchanges constitute communication and interaction between people, which among other things serves as a basis for social relations. Practices create *practice-*

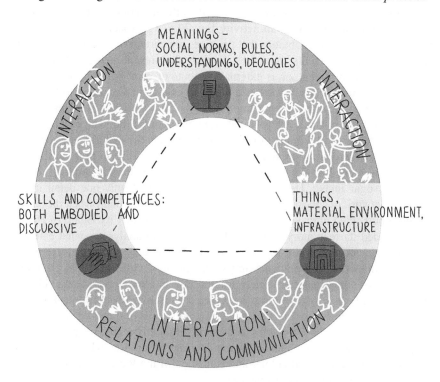

Figure 2.6   Composition of social practices (adapted from Shove et al., 2012)

specific interactions. For example, if we look at a shopping trip of parents and children as a practice, we can see specific 'exchanges' that are recognisable as 'typical' to these kinds of situations. Negotiating with a child over whether to buy a bottle of Coca-Cola or not is an example that combines parenting and shopping for food.

Sometimes it may be especially relevant to focus on these interactions to call forth social change. For example, a programme on consumer rights in Estonia initiated by the national Consumer Protection Board trained shopkeepers and salespeople to remind each buyer about the two-year product complaint period. Training was organised, information leaflets were sent to stores and the board's inspectors made 'undercover' control visits to shops in which they made purchases and if salespeople did not talk about the right to complain, the inspectors made detailed inquiries. This whole endeavour addressed a particular sales-situation interaction that was deemed crucial for consumers to know and defend their right-of-complaint more actively.

Think, stretch and sketch
Young adults take out excessive pay-day loans (speed credit) and end up with financial difficulties. Sketch the elements (meanings, skills and things) that support this problematic practice.

Different types of practices: in order to make the following section, which focuses on analysing practices for the sake of programme preparation, easier to grasp, some types of practices and their implications for programme design are proposed here. Behind this brief outline is an extensive, just emerging and exciting theoretical discussion. For the interested reader, references are given in the further reading list. We do not undervalue the importance of theory, yet the programme maker's life may often be compared to that of a fire-fighter, who has not much time, maybe none, to ponder deep conceptual issues, so we limit this to the basics only.

First of all, it is necessary to distinguish between *practices as performances* and as *entities* (Schatzki, 2002). The former are actual occurrences of activities as they transpire in reality. To recall the iceberg metaphor cited above, performances can be compared to behaviours, which are the visible part above the water and can be empirically analysed either in real time or retrospectively.

Yet a whole array of performances does not tell us much in itself. Practice as an entity – a meaningful whole that can be described in a recognisable way in a given socio-cultural setting – is the unit of analysis needed in social change programmes. Those entities need to change if we wish to achieve the new normality. Practices as entities have their own norms and rules. We can tell if an activity is a legitimate part of a practice or not (even if it is an innovative way of doing something) (see Warde, 2013). Thus the reader will have to – even if it proves to be a difficult task – delimit some practices as entities that are the main foci of his/her endeavours, because this keeps both the pre-programme analysis and implementation on track.

All practices are not the same, either empirically, when we look at their enactment in real life, or conceptually. Schatzki has proposed the useful notion of *integrative practices*: They are 'the more complex practices found in and constitutive of particular domains of social life, e.g., cooking, farming or business' (1996, p. 98). We may assume that some practices are 'tighter', more coordinated, than others (see Warde, 2013). This applies especially to work-related and formal practices that are documented and regulated by rules and instructions. For example, in our university department the ways of admitting new students each summer is a highly regulated area; there are formal procedures, tests, exams, interviews and admission criteria. Alan Warde (2013) has used the term 'coordinating agents' in this case. In an integrative practice, the sorts of agents – both human (e.g., management, professional bodies, sometimes even particular individuals) and non-human (e.g., technologies and documents) – that play key roles in maintaining a given network of activities must be identified. Those coordinating agents can be imagined as nodes in the socio-material network introduced above. A study-information system (which is nothing more than an information technology) of a university is a powerful non-human agent that coordinates the curricula, course time-tables and assessment of students. If a mark has not been entered into the system after a course is finished, the student's result does not exist, no matter how many months of tears and sweat have been put into writing papers, doings tests and submitting homework.

Thus we may say that those tightly organised integrative practices are in a sense 'high-density'. It may be easier to analyse such a dense practice because of its boundaries, rules and clarity. Yet such a practice may be harder to change because of the impenetrability of the network of practice coordination, both formal and informal.

It would be naive to think that all practices are well coordinated and easy to delimit, or even recognise. Warde (2013) elaborates on the concept of a *compound practice*. It muddies the waters here, but if we want to do justice to the complexity of real life, we must put that notion to work. According to Warde (2013), compound practices can be failed integrative practices that have not formed into full-blown well-coordinated practices, or they may be in the process of developing into more integration, but not yet there. His analysis focuses on eating, which has many aspects, and varies among cultures as well as within one culture. Warde points out: 'Performances of eating are, in the latter view, a complex corollary of the intersection of four, relatively autonomous integrative practices' (2013, p. 25). Eating is organised by many, sometimes even clashing, bodies and entities: a myriad of cookbooks, the food industry, organic farms, famous TV chefs, grocery shops, farmers' markets, dieticians, doctors etc. It is helpful to view such compound practices as having lower density and weaker coordination, although it makes them more difficult to analyse for obvious reasons. Maybe that is one of the reasons why the fight against obesity cannot boast global success so far. Eating is a very complex compound practice and eating 'wrong', in the sense of leading to weight gain, may happen in innumerable ways.

We can also call alcohol drinking as a whole a compound practice. Yet alcohol consumption by people in their daily lives manifests itself in hundreds of different ways. Is teenage excessive vodka drinking on a night when parents are away, with all its disastrous consequences of nasty hangovers, broken glasses and maybe even drunk driving, the same thing as having a glass of champagne with faculty on a sunny afternoon as part of a master's student's graduation celebration? Both are practices of alcohol drinking… yet not the same thing at all. Yet this is not to deny that loose compounds may sometimes consist of more tightly coordinated integrated sub-practices as it were, such as, in the above-described case, tightly controlled alcohol production and sales practices.

We may assume that compound practices, even though they are tricky to interpret, contain lower density spots, which are more accessible and responsive to interventions: such practices may – with good planning and some luck – be re-crafted into or replaced with more acceptable, desired ways of living. Also, within such compounds it may be possible to re-shape the interrelation of different practices. Because of weaker coordination, and more emergent and fluctuating status, there may be niches where a programme may enter and plant change in a meaningful and lasting manner.

Although individual behaviour-based thinking is still mainstream, some first attempts have been made to integrate behaviour and practice concepts in advice given to policy makers. A recent report for the European Commission (Umpfenbach, 2014), even though titled 'Influences on consumer behaviour. Policy implications beyond nudging', pays considerable homage to social practice theory-based research and acknowledges, for example, the importance of 'lock-ins' of consumers' behaviour, as well as the power of habit. Recommendations to policy makers proposed in the report are definitely worth consulting for inspiration, even though they seem to presume a relatively strong state hand in designing measures and levers to prompt more sustainable everyday life.

Another interesting source, which attempts to synthesise behaviour and practice-based accounts is the so-called ISM tool (I-individual, S-social, M-material) designed for the Scottish Government (Darnton and Horne, 2013). Even though it significantly also claims to move 'beyond' (the individual), it takes the behaviour as the basic 'unit' of intervention. However, considerable attention is paid to material and social aspects. Its strength is including other themes besides sustainable consumption (e.g., health, driving safety). While being quite a wide-ranging analytic guide (although for purist practice-theory proponents the mix of individual behaviour and social practice is still rather awkward here), its actual advice on how to design an intervention programme is compressed into one box in a ten-step guide, titled 'take action'. This handbook unpacks that box in much greater detail hoping to give some down-to-earth guidance on which concrete moves could be made by programme initiators, who may or, more likely, may not have great reservoirs of resources and political support at their disposal.

2.4 Summary

The preceding theoretical discussion has demonstrated that social practices are sites where agents (individuals) go about their daily lives, both enabled and constrained by social structure. Practices as social patterns of action lie in-between agents and structure and can be understood as a bridge between individuals or groups and socially constituted institutional and material conditions, resources, social meanings and norms.

A rational individual who consciously plans actions and whose free will alone can bring about social change is rare. Instead, a powerful stream of social theory focusing on social practices proposes to concentrate on patterns of action as the targets of change. This means asking the basic question: why and how do people do what they do?

The programme designer needs to think about practices-as-entities as analytical categories. Of course, in order to determine which practices-as-entities are the keys in the chosen territory, an analysis of behaviours or practices as performances has to be conducted. More on this can be found in the next chapter. Yet, it is crucial to bear in mind that these observable behaviours are only the tip of the iceberg; one must not limit social change programmes to trying to influence behaviours alone, neglecting the underlying social patterns that configure individual activities.

Practices consist of meanings, competences, materials and social interaction as an integrating dynamic between these elements, as well as between different practices that often intersect and overlap.

There are different types of practices: integrative and compound. The first can be understood in terms of higher-density and stronger coordination, which may make them easier to analyse, yet more challenging to change. Compound practices, which consist of different sub-practices on different levels of integration, are messier and much more difficult to make sense of: their boundaries are blurrier. This may in some situations make the programme designer's life easier by providing niches and 'holes' of lower-density and weaker coordination, making change more feasible.

In sum, although practice-based thinking does not deny the existence of the choosing and thinking individual, it proceeds from the assumption that in order to bring about social change, it is both useful and resource-saving not to delegate the whole burden of 'improving the world' to individual cognition. The key to change lies in the interwoven and mutual influence of both structural and individual factors.

The next chapters highlight how practices can be analysed, and how programme objectives can be set.

Further reading

Bertilsson, M. (1984). The theory of structuration: Prospects and problems. *Acta Sociologica* 27, 339–53. doi:10.1177/000169938402700404

Evans, D., McMeekin, A. and Southerton, D. (2012). Sustainable consumption, behaviour change policies and theories of practice. *COLLeGIUM: Studies Across Disciplines in the Humanities and Social Sciences* 12, 113–29. Retrieved from https://helda.helsinki.fi/handle/10138/34226

Giddens, A. (1984/1989). *The constitution of society: Outline of the theory of structuration*. Cambridge, England: Polity Press.

Schatzki, T.R. (1996). *Social practices: A Wittgensteinian approach to human activity and the social*. Cambridge, England: Cambridge University Press.

Shove, E., Pantzar, M. and Watson, M. (2012). *The dynamics of social practice. Everyday life and how it changes*. London: Sage.

Chapter 3
Preparing a social change programme

This chapter puts theoretical knowledge to work in actual programme preparation. The text and illustrations walk the reader through problem analysis in people's everyday lives (utilising tools that draw on sociological thinking about social practices), setting objectives for practice change, analysis of key actors in the field (more traditionally defined as target groups and stakeholders) and building a coalition of different partners, since no programme alone can achieve a long-term impact. The chapter ends with a sketch of a possible example programme meant to illustrate different ways of picking a strategic path that paves the way for tactical planning and implementation. The aim is to provide a systematic, usable yet theoretically coherent roadmap of analysis and planning that should ensure that the programme is on the right track from the start.

3.1 Problem formulation

Today's world is highly complex: economic, political and scientific logics of argumentation and interrelations between relevant institutions are multi-layered, so much so that their mutual interaction produces many subsidiary problems. Such terms as 'complexity-aware' and 'complexity-worthy' have been coined to train practitioners to cope with open situations and dynamic contexts (Beautement and Broenner, 2011). Complexity-worthiness can be compared to sea-worthiness, i.e., capable of coping with stormy seas (Beautement and Broenner, 2011). Such an attitude by and large conforms to the mindset of this book. This sensitises us to the change we wish to affect in our 'territory', which is part of a wider landscape where social situations relevant to the issue unfold. Such a point of departure invites programme makers to notice the constant flux of their own, their target groups', their partners' and other key actors' activities, as well as the dynamism of the whole environment.

Attempts to deal with one particular environmental or social risk may bring about a new one, as risks occur in cycles (Sapountzaki, 2010) and have mutual amplification and ripple effects. The division between tame and wicked problems clearly explicated by Sue McGregor (2011), based on the theory of complexity, is a useful tool in problem formulation. Wicked problems are closely linked with viewing the world as an open-ended flow of situations, not as a closed system. The following table juxtaposes these two vantage points, clearly encouraging the reader to tap into complexity instead of trying to do away with it, which is impossible anyway. As the table is entitled 'Ways of seeing', it doesn't focus on the ontological – how things are in the world – but on how we view the world and make sense of it. In the case of social change programmes, there actually aren't any genuinely tame problems or closed, predictable systems if we dig deep enough and do not engage in wishful thinking. So, if the reader recognises thinking based on the left-hand part of the table in reviewing her programme, this is a warning sign.

Table 3.1   Comparison of two ways of seeing problems and situations

Tame problems and closed systems	Wicked problems and open situations
Nature of the programme designer's 'territory'	
Closed, 'fenced' and easily identifiable	Open-ended, with many evolving situations
Actors in the territory	
Can be easily identified, counted and analysed based on their functions, relation to the problem and characteristics	A varying number of actors with changing capabilities, roles and dynamic practices
Control and coordination of the territory	
Planning and direction of the systems and entities done by a single or a few coordinators, organisations	No single locus, organisation or agent which controls the territory, a continuum of agents with varying coordinating capability
Context of the problem	
Routine, predictable context	Dynamic context, ever-changing tension
Nature of the problem	
Clearly bounded, tame, identifiable roots and consequences. A problem may be complex and technically detailed but there is a consensus that a solution can be found	Wicked, a bundle of problems intertwined with each other, difficult to structure and very complex, involving many different actors; the consequences may be global and unpredictable and bring about various risks
Ways of thinking towards a solution	
Reductionist thinking that divides the problem into parts possible; clear solutions possible. Can be solved by using expert knowledge in a certain sphere	Common-sense, holistic thinking. Expert knowledge in a certain sphere is not sufficient; local knowledge based on the immediate experience of the people concerned is required
Process of finding a solution	
Relatively easy structured methods based on expert knowledge followed to find definitive solutions	Approaches/heuristics depending on the context, local knowledge, constant 'translation' between different interests. Temporary and changing solutions.
Transferability of solutions	
An old solution can fit a new problem	Each problem is unique and a solution that has been used earlier may not be transferable or up-scalable.

Actors' relation to the solution	
Everybody agrees that there is a solution; interpretation of a solution can be consensual	Interpretations of solutions (whatever qualify as solutions) vary; selecting difficult due to different interests and difficulty of dialogue (constant need for 'translation')
Consequences	
The consequences of solutions are predictable within the territory and landscape	The consequences of solutions are unpredictable because each solution can create new wicked problems. Even if consequences are as expected in the given territory of the problem/programme, they may produce unpredictable side-effects related to some other problem/territory

Adapted from McGregor (2011: 64) and Beautement and Broenner (2011: 17–18)

Think and stretch

Think about each problem. Is it a wicked or a tame problem? Why do you think so?
1. Children's obesity and the increase in related health expenditures.
2. Every year a lot of baby deer perish in fields during mowing: tractors move from the outside to the inside of fields and deer are trapped in the middle of the fields.

The 'nudge' approach referred to in the first chapter implicitly assumes that problems are tame or can be tamed, i.e., can be solved by using expert knowledge, can be bound in at least temporarily closed systems, and that consequences or solutions are predictable. In most cases, programmes that seek change are necessitated by wicked problems involving many different interested parties and for which there are no single immediate solutions. That is why the social practice approach is proposed here: it deals with the complexity of everyday life.

Sometimes it is helpful to draw a problem tree following a hierarchy principle: problems are related to each other through causes and consequences, i.e., causes are lower level problems, while consequences are new problems caused by the core problem. This also assists in determining specific objectives.

How problems are phrased in institutional or specialist language is usually not understandable to lay people. The first step is to express issues (usually there is no single problem but a set of intertwined themes) in the language of everyday practices. Some topics can be expressed clearly with the help of statistics, research reports, opinion surveys, expert opinions etc. Let's take adult drowning as an example. Nobody intends to drown: we may say that such activities are not 'listed in our daily repertoire' (excluding suicide). Thus, the solution cannot be formulated as 'do not drown', but must be related to what people actually do at lakes, rivers and the seashore. The statistics of adult drowning show that men are at risk more than women (World Health Organization, 2014). Male drowning incidents are often related to leisure activities at the waterside (see National Water Safety Forum, 2013). Thus the problem, when looked at from the viewpoint of people's everyday life, can be phrased in a new way: relaxing at the waterside is a problematic practice because it creates the temptation to go swimming without proper self-evaluation, due to peer group influence and/or while drinking alcohol (World Health Organization, 2014). Visualisation of the topic may guide in transforming an abstract, institutionally determined problem into an everyday life context, because it is easier and more comprehensible to the viewer to imagine particular activities, things and environments than abstract statements. Figure 3.1 presents the problem of young men drowning.

Figure 3.1   Formulation of the problematic practice

The next step is delineation of the desired ways of thinking and doing in order to reduce the number of lost lives. One solution is to warn people. To say in a robust way: 'Do not swim when drunk', using warning signs or social advertisements (see Figure 3.2).

But does simply warning not to swim when drunk really work? In everyday life a problematic action often consists of *non-doings* (people do not think about risks at a party) or *co-doings* (it is customary for young people to drink at parties at the seashore). Also, alcohol may make people more optimistic about their swimming skills and more forgetful about self-monitoring.

Thus the alternative solution is to encourage collective safeguarding: to persuade people to look after each other, hoping that they then are also more responsible in their own behaviour. The call to restrain friends from going into the water when they are drunk constructs another type of duty that concerns in-group relationships and requires good social skills, because the reactions of peers may be negative. It is also more sensitive towards general cultural norms: friendship, norms of public behaviour, personal autonomy etc. This strategy has been implemented in Estonia for three years, but it is too early to evaluate long-term change. Studies (e.g., Trink, 2015) indicate that the above-mentioned suggestion is closely related to whether the habit of monitoring the activities of friends at a party is established in friendship groups. Currently about every second young male in the sample reports that in his peer group looking after friends at parties is normal. Swimming at parties occurs only for a relatively short time in summer, whereas

Figure 3.2   **Social advertisement 'Do not swim when drunk' and an informal traffic sign informing of the dangers of drunk swimming**

Reprinted with the permission of the Estonian Rescue Board

parties are arranged all year round. Thus in order to recruit more actors into this 'friend-obstruction' the more general habit of monitoring friends at any party and at any time might be needed. The actualisation of one particular 'seasonal' danger may not have a sustainable effect in establishing the general observation practice. Time will tell whether the re-crafting of young men's party habits is successful or not.

Think and stretch

How would you word the following statement as (a) problematic social practice(s)? 'Obesity costs this country about $150 billion a year, or almost 10 per cent of the national medical budget. Approximately one in three adults and one in six children are obese. Obesity is now epidemic in the United States and a major cause of death attributable to heart disease, cancer and diabetes' (National Center for Chronic Disease Prevention and Health Promotion, 2011).

Thinking about social problems through the prism of social practices is not always as obvious as in the example above. Therefore we advise not automatically adopting problem definitions of officials and experts. Many problems are institutional constructs unconnected with everyday life. For example, food risks and energy sustainability are globally very important issues concerning people's everyday lives. But we go to the grocery store to 'provision the family with foodstuffs', i.e., to buy food, not to 'do risk-avoiding' by keeping away from pesticides and additives. The (non)consumption of something is rarely an action per se, but rather a prerequisite or an (unwanted) side-effect of some other action or social relationship. Thus, if we want to change our amounts or ways of consumption, we have to address these 'other' actions and relationships, and the related things, skills and meanings. Research on electricity usage has shown that despite technological improvements (low-energy houses and domestic appliances, smart grids etc.), consumer lifestyles and the logic of everyday actions still have a strong impact on actual electricity usage (Gram-Hanssen, 2013). Electricity usage is not fully governed by either economic or environmental concerns, even when awareness levels and technical circumstances are very favourable (Røpke and Christensen, 2013). Researchers argue that opportunities to solve energy consumption problems by increasing the number of 'aligned consumers', who act rationally, responsibly and sustainably, does not depend as much on better feedback, guidance and training, or smart gadgets for self-monitoring and decision-making as on lifestyle as a whole (Gram-Hanssen, 2013; Shove and Walker, 2014). Excessive electricity consumption is a problem in the engineer's world, but lay people do not 'consume' electricity: for them it is something invisible that underlies various everyday activities, from watching TV to storing food in a freezer.

The aligned consumer and risk-aware citizen are ideal constructs only within the institutional, expert logic of definition and framing. Therefore, evocations to be more vigilant and exercise more (self-)monitoring may have only a fleeting effect: without reiteration, people forget and switch back to business as usual.

Thus programme calls to action should build upon 'natural frames' that provide support. Earlier, a social change programme was compared to a perennial plant. Its initiators and implementers are like gardeners who plan to introduce a new plant and have to consider which type of soil suits best, and whether direct sunlight or shade is more favourable. To some extent, it is possible to enhance conditions, e.g., use a fertilizer. But if the location seems unfavourable, it may be wiser to try another plant (i.e., design a different programme). The next sub-chapter gives guidance on how to analyse problems and environments.

3.2 Analysing everyday lives in context: types and components of practices

In Chapter 2, section 2.2, the well-known iceberg metaphor was referred to in describing social practices: problematic behaviours are only the tip of the iceberg, whereas the whole social and material network that configures the problematic behaviour is hidden under the water (Spurling et al., 2013). Designing a programme without examining this hidden part may lead to only transitory effects, because only the surface of the problem is dealt with. The visible section can be illustrated by statistical indicators (e.g., the number of people seeking professional help), ratios (e.g., the number of HIV-positive individuals per thousand people) or international indices (e.g., alcohol consumption by countries). The aim of the analysis outlined here is to make the underlying network known and understandable, as well as map within this network the particular territory an intervention can feasibly cover.

For example, school bullying is a social problem illustrated by anonymous surveys (e.g., Ditch the Label Anti-Bullying Charity, 2014), the number of students who have sought counselling and the number of conflicts in schools. But what are the social practices that lead to it? Is it a distorted form of collective identity-building (boundary-making between 'us' and the 'other')? Or is it a cruel practice of relationship formation (bullies get admirers)? Or perhaps an imitation of an adult power establishment (e.g., mental bullying)? Or just a violent expression of school stress without any special goals? Bullying performances may emerge as by-products of other practices of school life, such as participation in classes and spending time during breaks, that are *socially coordinated* (Warde, 2013) by rules and curricula, unwritten conventions, penalties and rewards for good performance, and individual or institutional authorities. Bullying may be a result of weak coordination of certain activity patterns. For example, a school may have a code of conduct and rules that encourage respect for others, but such rules may be overlooked all too often. Warde (2013) calls this a state of weak coordination. In some cases bullying might not be an occasional consequence of an unfortunate configuration of teaching, parenting, school managing etc., but a practice on its own that is re-established with particular rituals, places, artefacts etc.

To diagnose bullying in a particular area, school(s), age groups etc., we suggest drawing up a likely socio-material network of school life, by marking possible relevant institutional and individual actors, rules, things and physical rooms that –

Figure 3.3   School spaces as parts of the socio-material network
Photo by Kadri Ugur

perhaps mostly unintentionally – enable school violence to emerge and persist, as mutually interconnected nodes in the network.

The following section is meant to explain how to conduct the above-mentioned analysis. Next, we provide a list of categories that need to be addressed. We strongly recommend also mapping the nexus visually: putting the problematic practice at the centre and drawing the nexus with relevant meaningful nodes around it.

School bullying has been extensively researched and numerous prevention efforts have been made in different countries. Referring to some of them, we sketch a hypothetical socio-material network (see Figure 3.3). The same basic model can be used to explore different problems. To facilitate analysis, it is advisable to divide it into parts, indicating the different types of affecting factors.

Physical or virtual environment and things: One should first focus on buildings, interiors and organisation of space. Actual or virtual (participatory) observation – site-visits and close observation (if possible) of the target group – may be necessary.

In the case of school bullying, it is vital to understand the architecture of the school building(s). Are there any hidden corners? Studies indicate that especially younger children (Cunningham et al., 2010) are afraid of quiet and dark corners that remain out of the sight and hearing of teachers. Such places can be found in most schools and the stronger the supervision, the more bullies try to lure their victims into such areas. The solution is to illuminate, redesign or secure the lonely corners. However, constant patrolling does not remove the causes of the problem and there is a risk that as soon as supervision relaxes, bullying will start again.

Think and stretch
Look at Figure 3.3. How may this school space contribute to creating and maintaining bullying practice(s)?

The next question is: *how much are pupils allowed to move around the school during breaks?* Children get tired and are faced with great mental stress that may be relieved by teasing others if there is nothing else to do. Instead of constant monitoring of children (which may cause more tension), they should be offered physical activities that reduce stress (op. cit.). *Are there any security systems (cameras) in place?* Many schools have installed security cameras, which create the feeling of control.

Economic-material resources also require attention in any background analysis. The main theme here is the availability or lack of money and time because intangible resources will also materialise eventually. Financial documents, expert interviews and observations are valuable data sources. This aspect closely links with social relations, for example, the possibility of using unpaid volunteers. However, the question arises: does the school have the *means to hire a social worker, a psychologist and a security guard?* As children are often mocked or bullied due to their appearance or clothes, pupils believe that compulsory *school uniforms* could be a solution, but that requires additional expenditure by parents.

Rules, regulations, job descriptions and unwritten responsibilities of certain positions are important indicators of practice coordination. Examination of legal documents, written rules and instructions, oral mentoring (e.g., for new students), recruitment interview guides and information collected in internal information systems provide insights. They shed light on which activities are favoured and which ones are discouraged, on the hierarchy and rationale of actions. A statute as a basic document or an information system that archives students' marks, teacher feedback and communication with parents can be seen as coordinating agents that set the boundaries of practices, make certain activities and utterances possible and rule others out as forbidden, unacceptable or technically too cumbersome.

Actions of bullies are disapproved of and usually prohibited by the internal rules of schools and at a higher level by laws. But this may not be enough. Regulation of the responsibilities and rights of teachers is crucial. If teachers' job descriptions establish that they are paid only for contact hours, it is difficult to motivate them to keep an eye on pupils during breaks, to co-operate with other teachers and to organise extracurricular activities.

Internal procedures of schools prescribe how the handling of problems is organised and communicated. Does it happen *ad hoc* or is it standardised? In the US, some schools have established 'peace negotiations' between feuding parties (the children themselves) instead of external intervention by adults, i.e., punishment (Morrison and Vaandering, 2012).

Timetables and curricula are powerful organisers of school rhythms. Pupils (Cunningham et al., 2010) have said that spending the whole day with the same classmates creates a stressful environment. Fixed power relations are strengthened, and alternative qualities or skills of pupils are not noticed. Mixing children helps them to make new friends through different activities and based on different features and interests. Thus the rigid timetable of classes is a powerful coordinating agent that impedes mingling and versatility. In addition, the existence of a system and tradition of extracurricular activities and events, where children can meet, may be a coordinator of bullying practice: preventing or supporting it.

Meanings: Problem practices are always in some way related to more general social norms, values and understandings. For example, intense competition and a success-oriented mentality in schools and in society as a whole may encourage school violence. However, an entire school or a particular group of teachers can work out professional standards for teamwork-supporting methods and didactics in order to develop co-operative and respectful relations between pupils. Such cases may become models for others to follow. For example, some US schools make their environments friendlier and less competitive through word games defining common values (Morrison and Vaandering, 2012). In a similar vein, if the general understanding in society about school violence is individual-centred, with the causes of bullying seen as lying mainly in the psyche of the individual victim or the bully, such a viewpoint prevents collective discussions on the topic. This is because the problem is framed as an individual failing, not as a collective social pattern of activity that has an inner logic of its own, independent of individual cases and students.

Interaction and relations: In general, one should examine what mechanisms shape relations between relevant groups. What are the possibilities and habits of interaction? Does the problem behaviour facilitate the formation of hierarchies? How does the problem practice spread? All this often boils down to simple questions of how people meet, what they do together, what they talk about and which channels of communication they use. Often practice-specific interactions, e.g., certain forms of conversation between people, whether face-to-face or mediated (e.g., via social media), are used and make sense in the context of the coherence of a set of activities. With bullying, there are certain specific ways in which the violent episodes erupt, certain ways in which words are uttered and bodies move. Although direct observation in such sensitive cases can be next to impossible, it is crucial to get information on how people interact in such situations. However, to comprehend the details of problem situations, it is important to scrutinize a wider interactional context: which rituals are observed at school? What kind of relations prevail between teachers? To what extent and how are parents involved in school life? If information is exchanged only through formal, school-initiated channels (e.g., through the class teacher or a website), interaction between parents and their contribution to problem solving are limited.

Skills, competences and know-how: In the context of the present example, skills can refer to the ways various parties respond to violent incidents. How do the eye-witnesses behave? Do they have relevant knowledge and skills for the performance? Do the teachers know how to react? One programme that has been effective in reducing bullying, according to a large randomised controlled trial (Laitinen, 2012), is called KIVA (in translation something like 'Cool!', but also an acronym for 'bullying-free' in Finnish). It has been used in Finland (Future Learning Finland, n.d.), by the University of Turku, and is based on the fact that school violence is a cruel form of relationship building (Caravita et al., 2008; Cillessen and Borch, 2006; Juvonen and Galván, 2008). This explanation has been applied in other prevention programmes, but Prof. Salmivalli and her colleagues (2012) dug more deeply into the social architecture of bullying. They highlighted the crucial importance of onlookers/bystanders, who – by their silent presence – support bullying as a strategy to gain, maintain and increase status in the peer group. In their prevention programme, the main focus is on onlookers/bystanders, who are trained not to offer silent support to offenders.

Figure 3.4   **Visualisation of the socio-material network that enables bullying and the territory of a particular programme to deal with it**

The network of these social and material elements is shown in Figure 3.4. In order to carry out analysis on particular countries or schools, the nodes of the network should naturally be adapted and complemented. Components of the network contribute to constructing everyday micro-situations that reinforce or prevent bullying. Systematic changes in these, in turn, increase or decrease the occurrence of bullying. A change in the number and substance of the nodes in the network – for example, introducing school uniforms and 'mixing' of children – reshapes the school environment and changes the atmosphere. This is much more complicated than organising an anti-bullying event or preparing a supervision schedule for teachers. The results, however, are likely to be more durable. Thus the first step is to identify institutions, rules, material circumstances etc. that may contribute to problematic practices (represented as nodes of the network), and institutional and individual actors who are directly involved in or mediate actions that may support or hinder the emergence, persistence and communication of the problematic action (e.g., teachers and social workers). The second step is to mark the potential programme's *own territory*: the most relevant nodes and key actors the particular programme aims to target: these are marked in bold in Figure 3.4.

In the next section we discuss change strategies.

3.3 Setting objectives for the programme: planning a long-term impact

The practice-centred problem analysis is focused mainly on context and interaction and less on linear processes, individuals and groups. Unlike the conventional logic of preparing a programme, the overall objective of our approach is somewhat wider than defining the specific target group and messages directed to them. Visually speaking, we have (re)designed a pattern, (re)cultivated the garden. For self-sustaining change, we have to re-shape something in the chosen territory within the socio-material network. Whereas the 'nudge' approach treats members of society as passive participants who follow scripts programmed by experts and internalise the signals communicated by the system, we assume that any social change programme re-designs some part(s) – even if tiny ones – of the social structure that both constrains and enables the activities of individual actors. Based on the Giddensian concept of structuration, we assume that social change occurs when re-configuration of the socio-material network opens up new possibilities for agency: individual or institutional actors' relationship to rules and resources changes. Either they can follow the rules or use the resources better (they have become more accessible and significant), modify the rules or improve the workings of resource production and distribution (e.g., through co-creation).

Members of the British Sustainable Practices Research Group suggest practice-based problem framings (Spurling et al., 2013) that propose setting objectives in a non-linear and open-ended environment. Based on this, we elaborated their typology further and connected it with a diagnosis of a particular socio-material network. In doing this we drew upon the theoretical concepts of *integrative* and *compound practices,* expounded in Chapter 2, section 2.3. In real life the setting of objectives and analysis of the territory of a problematic practice do not follow each other linearly, but are often intertwined and undertaken in parallel or alternately.

Creating new practices: This is a good strategy when we operate in the context of *compound practices* that are weakly coordinated. This does not necessarily mean that the socio-material network is hostile, but the imagined territory of potential change can be characterised as having low density of coordination, which permits a multitude of varying performances (see Figure 3.7).

For example, in most countries roads have reflectors that help drivers stay on the road, notice barriers etc. But how the visibility of pedestrians in the dark is coordinated and regulated varies significantly from country to country. In some societies pedestrians are required to make themselves visible to other road users in the dark or in poor daylight conditions by wearing reflective outdoor clothing or shoes or carrying reflective materials, but in many countries safe walking in the dark is not regulated at all.

In Estonia wearing small hanging reflectors or reflective ribbons affixed to outerwear is a specific practice. The Estonian Road Administration persuades and reminds people to wear small hanging reflectors each autumn, when it gets dark early. Special media campaigns have been carried out since 2005. Advertisements

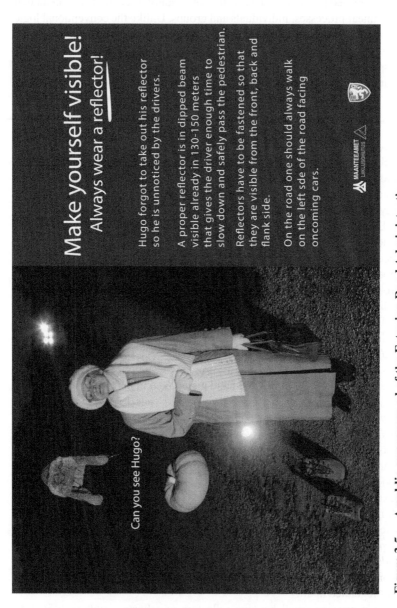

Figure 3.5   A public awareness ad of the Estonian Road Administration
Reprinted with permission of the Estonian Road Administration

Figure 3.6   Small wearable reflectors have various shapes and purposes: they may express aesthetic values as ornaments or functional value as key rings

Photo by Aare Abrams

feature various visual and verbal tactics to motivate people to use this simple item (see Figure 3.5).

In other campaigns people are asked to remind their loved ones to wear reflectors. Practical training exercises are arranged in schools and social welfare institutions. Demonstrations show how late a driver notices a pedestrian in dark clothes, how brief the time to react is and, in contrast, at what distance a pedestrian wearing a reflector is seen. In addition these small items are distributed to pedestrians by traffic police patrols at night on streets and highways. A special website was created where people could donate money and thus provide their friends or whole village communities with these little life-saving devices. It was assumed that receiving a gift would have a greater impact. The website made such gift giving convenient and the packages were delivered by the Estonian Postal Service.

The socio-material network of road safety made the creation of such a pedestrian visibility practice easily adoptable. Estonian traffic regulations require road pedestrians to use reflectors in the dark. This has motivated suppliers to comply with technical standards for material (the surface should make the wearer visible in a car headlights' beam 130 to 150 metres away) and employ this message in their marketing to stress the high quality of their products.

The coalition partners of the campaign are shops who sell reflectors and remind buyers with special point-of-sale promotions. The material aspects of the item itself are significant: low production cost, many different shapes and sizes, and aesthetic usability. Reflectors have become popular objects (see Figure 3.6) as ornaments, souvenirs and corporate gifts. Entertainment entrepreneurs offer decorate-your-reflector courses etc. Due to these factors, a new practice of wearing reflectors has taken root in Estonia and has also been exported to other countries.

Modification of existing practices: This can be advisable in a context where the boundaries of practices are more clear-cut but the level of their coordination is still not very high (see Figure 3.7). The imagined territory usually covers both 'good' and more problematic performances that exist side-by-side in more or less tense interrelationships. Empowering agents who practise 'good' forms of performance may help to accelerate the formation of a desired integrative practice. For example, in order to support environmentally sustainable practices, Spurling et al. advise: 'reduce the resource-intensity' of performance (2013, p. 5). This may be accomplished by changing the materials, competences and meanings (Shove et al., 2012).

For example, in alcohol abuse prevention programmes people are instructed to monitor the alcohol units they consume and not exceed the allowed amount. But an alcohol unit is a rather abstract construct that is difficult to monitor while drinking. In many countries special web pages offer tools to calculate these units but using these requires extra knowledge and effort. When producers are obliged to print how many alcohol units a certain bottle or can contains, the self-monitoring process becomes more accessible. For example, in the UK the

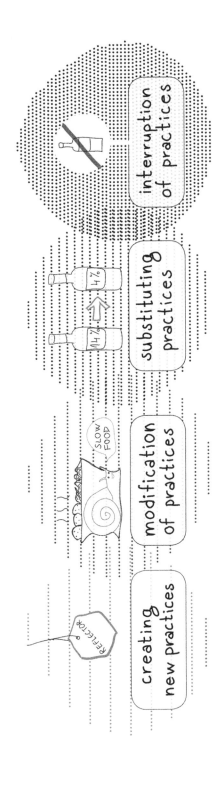

Figure 3.7 Types of practice changes as aims of the social change programme

majority of relevant companies have joined the Public Health Responsibility Deal led by the governmental Department of Health and have pledged to display the number of units on at least 80 per cent of drink containers (UK Department of Health, n.d.). Certainly the socio-material network that shapes drinking habits contains many more rules, habits, institutions etc. that coordinate drinking in a particular country or social group. The bottle-marking action is one part of a bigger programme of fostering a culture of responsible drinking within the official guidelines (Drinkaware, n.d.) that the government has established in co-operation with the business sector. We discuss this programme further in the next subsection, 'substituting practices'.

Think and stretch

Think of the organisation you work for. Pick a practice that is especially high density, tightly documented and regulated. What coordinates (i.e., regulates, maintains) this practice? What would it take to change the practice?

Spurling et al. differentiate, as a specific type of problem-framing, change in 'the complex interactions between practices' (2013, p. 5). The underlying idea is that the way in which practices are related to each other, how they intersect, generates the power that 'recruits' actors, and creates the logic and inevitability for people to behave in certain ways. The aim of interventions in such cases is to re-position the elements that make up these relationships, shift the centres, re-configure the nodes of the network etc. The Slow Food movement (see http://www.slowfood.com) aims to bond cooking with interacting with friends and family, treating meal preparation as quality time spent with close ones.

The 'Help! I want to save a life!' marrow donors' registry kit inside a box of bandages connects in a simple way to other practices: when we cut ourselves, we search for a bandage. In order to register as a donor, a blood sample and registration document are needed. However, the process itself was very complicated in the US due to bureaucratic rules and institutional procedures (Douglas, n.d.). The kit links two practices. A simple marrow donor registration form and an envelope are included in the package of over-the-counter bandages and, when people use them, they also can easily take a sample of blood, fill in the form and enclose it in a prepaid envelope (see Figure 3.8). This modification united two practices that already existed in a novel way. This required some, but not fundamental, alterations in the institutional arrangements of donor registration, manufacturing and packaging of appropriate items for blood sampling and registration that meet the legal, medical etc. standards of the country. All this was augmented by a Cannes award-winning advertising campaign. This initiative increased the donor registration rate significantly (Douglas, n.d.).

Figure 3.8   Marrow donor registration kit: equipment for taking a blood sample, registration notice and bandages

Reprinted with the permission of Graham Douglas

Substituting Practices: The next strategy is one of substituting practices. Spurling and colleagues (2013) describe the objective – in the sustainability context – as follows: replacing less sustainable practices with more sustainable alternatives. This strategy springs from rather similar general conditions: in order to substitute something, practices need to be rather well coordinated, but still not very dense, to allow space for changes in the socio-material network that they are embedded in (see Figure 3.7). The substitute rarely has identical functions and meanings to the original: it will re-work relationships with other practices and between people. The issue is whether these accompanying effects are tolerable and whether they shift the process in the desired direction. Major side-effects may remain hidden at first.

Therefore, we suggest involving beneficiaries and coalition partners in co-creation activities and testing a substitution on smaller samples under different conditions.

Social change programmes may also offer partial substitutions. For example, the responsible drinking programme of the UK Department of Health (n.d.), referred to above, aims not to stop drinking alcohol fully, but to keep it within reasonable limits and thereby aims to replace strong alcohol drinks with drinks containing less alcohol. In order to facilitate consumer choice of such products, the programme encourages alcohol suppliers to develop attractive alternatives: new light alcohol brands. Such a strategy is more tolerable than total prohibition both culturally (drinks as a part of socialising practices) and economically, because of the win–win relationship with businesses: the suppliers get increased revenue by creating new lower alcohol brands. The results have been positive: lighter alcohol sales are climbing and the number of people whose alcohol intake remains within the official weekly limits has increased (Wilson, 2013).

Another, often-cited example is the CoolBiz programme in Tokyo, which was launched to reduce carbon emissions. Here the earlier standard of 22°C room temperature in governmental offices, which was maintained artificially by heating in winter and cooling in summer, was replaced with a more flexible framework, between 20 and 28 °C. That necessitated revising office clerks' clothing habits, special lighter clothing brands were launched, and fashion shows were held that encouraged abandoning jackets and suits on hot summer days. The effect was a drop in carbon emissions by 1.7 million tonnes. But this effect was limited and therefore criticised (Shove et al., 2012), because the old building standards that foresaw indoor temperatures between 22 and 24° C all year round still remained in place.

It is never possible to foresee all risks or setbacks. Nevertheless, it is advisable to include test periods and test sites when planning substitutions in order to learn what side-effects the planned changes may cause and how they can be handled.

Disruption of unwanted/problematic practices: In addition to the strategies identified by Spurling and colleagues (2013), we propose a fourth. *Disruption* means that the socio-material network in which a practice is embedded is dismantled more or less completely. This is mostly applicable in the context of high density (see Figure 3.7), when we want to get rid of undesirable, but tightly coordinated, culturally rooted integrative practices. Cases in which only institutional interventions are enough to disrupt or abolish a deeply rooted practice are rare, but there are some emergency situations or circumstances of cultural, economic or social upheaval where this may be possible.

In such situations a modification or replacement strategy may not be sufficient to catalyse change – considerable inertia and resistance by various social actors, as well as from practices as patterns of activity, are likely. Schatzki argues in explaining this inertia of dense systems: 'It is in part because so much hangs together with them that high level ends do not change often in social life' (2013, p. 34). Therefore, one may easily decide in favour of a more revolutionary approach that interrupts the established inertia in order to achieve a social change. However, a high risk of unexpected or unwanted outcomes prevails.

An internationally well-known example of the disruption of practice is an alcohol ban in which the production, delivery and sale of alcohol is prohibited by law. The first bans date back to ancient times. At the beginning of the twentieth century, when alcohol consumption increased considerably, bans were enacted in several Western[1] countries: the USA, Canada, Australia, Russia, Finland, Sweden, Norway, Iceland, Russia and elsewhere. The implementation of 'dry laws' often enjoyed wide public legitimacy, with referenda being connected with temperance movements, political empowerment of women and civic movements (Blocker et al., 2003; Herlihy, 2002). For example, in Finland prohibition was among the first acts after independence from the Russian Empire, after several earlier failures due to opposition from the tsar (Sulkunen, 1991). The conditions of the time were favourable for this political and economic decision. It also produced numerous unwanted side-effects, such as bootlegging with accompanying violence, a crime rate surge and secret consumption. Partly because of this, and partly because of an altered economic and political environment (economic depression and war), repeals were introduced.

Alcohol consumption has long been a target of less radical interventions. For example, Mikhail Gorbachev introduced a rather systematic anti-alcohol policy in the Soviet Union when he came to power in 1985. After decades of a very liberal alcohol policy in the 50s and 60s, alcohol consumption increased and there were some erratic attempts to limit it in the 70s (Arusaar-Tamming, 2007). Gorbachev's new stricter policy limited the sale of alcoholic beverages both in terms of amounts and times of sale. The amounts were regulated by coupons that were issued to inhabitants each month (see Figure 3.9), with additional amounts permitted for weddings and funerals. Any consumption at organisational functions, even a glass of champagne at an official reception, was forbidden. Alcohol consumption was also prohibited on official and public premises. People recall that when parties, birthdays, funerals or weddings were held on official premises, alcohol was kept in jugs and consumed from juice glasses (see Figure 3.10). Increases in prices of alcoholic beverages and stricter penalties for illegal sales and use of alcohol were also part of the policy (Arusaar-Tamming, 2007). The disruption of drinking practices was done not only with sales restrictions. Special efforts were also made to support alternative recreational activities: sports activities, as well as an increase in the availability of various (male) hobby-related goods, such as carpentry tools, spare parts for cars and motorcycles, etc. In order to discourage the practice of individual wine making from home-grown berries and apples, various institutions

---

1 In many Asian and Islamic countries, such as Saudi Arabia, Bangladesh and Libya, alcohol is banned, but there the laws have a strong historical-religious background. Thus there is no disruption of existing alcohol production and consumption practices. For that reason, the alcohol ban as a disruption of established practices is discussed mainly in the context of North American and European countries.

Figure 3.9   Coupon for buying alcohol (one bottle of vodka, brandy or liqueur, or two bottles of wine). The coupon had to be used during December 1988

Reprinted with the permission of the Museum of Hiiumaa. Photo by Urmas Liit

were obliged to buy these potential raw materials from citizens. Also, the system of paying salaries was changed to reduce the temptation to 'celebrate' pay-days with alcohol (Arusaar-Tamming, 2007). Alcohol consumption decreased from 10.9 litres of pure alcohol per capita to 9.8 litres in 1985, to 7.5 litres in 1986 and to 6.4 litres in 1987. Gorbachev was forced to loosen the alcohol policy due to economic pressure in 1988, but consumption did not increase to the previous high levels (Arusaar-Tamming, 2007).

Despite a few vehement proponents of prohibition of alcohol for the sake of public health, the idea of a total ban has repercussions for many other practices that make up the current political and economic system, as well as the cultural foundations of the modern Western world, consumer sovereignty and freedom of enterprise being its pillars. A total alcohol ban is exercised in countries where historical and religious traditions strongly support it.

A large-scale disruption of practices usually occurs with major political and economic reforms in a society or a change in regimes. Transition societies

Figure 3.10   Photo of an initiation party in the Department of History, (State) University of Tartu in autumn 1987, staff table. As the party took place on official premises, alcohol had to be consumed covertly. Some jugs on the table contained alcohol and others non-alcoholic beverages. Some people had two glasses in front of them, one for non-alcoholic drinks and one for alcoholic drinks
Story by Anu Järs (the Estonian National Museum), photo from her private archive

have faced a multitude of such interruptions, with both positive and negative consequences for different population groups. The experience of post-Socialist transformation societies has shown various forms of social *inertia* that make practices shift back to their original forms. Thus when applying the disruption strategy the key question is how to recruit the creative potential of institutions, collectives and individuals to interpret change in a way that fosters the desired end, to make the change meaningful (even if disliked). Omar Lizardo and Michael Strand (2010) argue that in a situation where individuals' practical expectations are severely disappointed and they feel limited institutional support and external guidance for action, they are very open to new counter-ideologies. Thus it is crucial to offer enough support and guidance to keep the counter-ideologies at bay, but still maintain the creative potential of actors.

Our own research has also demonstrated that doing mundane things in a novel manner can be adopted quickly, although thinking patterns tend to be very inertial (Keller and Vihalemm, 2015). Our ethnographic research on how lower-income people in Estonia coped with the changeover to the euro revealed not much difficulty in learning new currency rates and handling bank notes and coins. Lower-income consumers were used to paying in cash at grocery stores, but after the coming of the euro they started using bank cards because the euro coins were difficult to deal with. The new payment habit, however, also did away with previous informal record keeping based on counting cash (and separating it into portions for different purposes). Some institutional guidance and support of record keeping of electronic money is provided by such governmental organisations as the web page Minuraha (My Money), online tools for keeping track of expenses offered by commercial banks etc. (http://www.minuraha.ee). However, partly because of weak promotion and partly because of the general price rises, people did not learn to use these facilitators. They felt unable to control their expenses and this seriously compromised their dignity as proper citizens who paid taxes and avoided debt (Keller and Vihalemm, 2015).

Many interruptions to lifestyle are not intentional but are due to the macro-level political or economic rationale, with changes in peoples' everyday life being an inevitable by-product. The disruption of existing habits as an intentional strategy can occur not only through changing laws or major political-economic reforms but also in minor changes, e.g., in funding principles. Initiators of social change are themselves involved in the process, and their own practices change during the programme. This can sometimes boost a reform in the very ways projects are carried out. Donors may re-work financing schemes in order to discontinue established ineffective practices of management and to force more efficient ones to be implemented. For example, instead of financing small scattered projects to educate youth about the natural environment, it is possible to develop nature education centres open to everybody at all times and offer quality programmes; instead of supporting expensive equipment purchases (e.g., binoculars) for one project, opening a special financing instrument for the purchase of equipment requiring that the buyers guarantee equipment access to other interested actors, e.g., non-commercial renting of binoculars (Estonian Environmental Investment Center, 2014).

Think and stretch

Which of the following objectives of alcohol policy are designed to prevent drinking, which are designed to re-shape habits and which are designed to create new practices?
Reducing total consumption of alcohol
Reducing alcohol abuse
Preventing alcohol consumption by minors
Reducing alcohol-related crime, social problems and health issues
Developing treatment and rehabilitation services to help motivate alcoholics to recover from their addiction

---

As everyday life is constantly changing, it is useful to have a 'buffer' so that it is possible to reformulate objectives as new information becomes available and the environment changes. In most cases, such revisions are tactical. An earlier detailed analysis of the social reality provides assurance that the strategic approach and the nuances that need to be adjusted are compatible.

3.4 Traditional and new ways of defining target groups and stakeholders

After or while setting the objectives of the programme, the target groups have to be selected from the performers of the practice who are believed to 'inhabit' the territory of the planned change, either as individual or collective actors (members of groups or organisations). Among project managers and communicators, the terms *target group* and *stakeholders* are familiar. For present purposes, we may define a *target group* as a group of individuals who are directly or indirectly involved in a practice, i.e., the people whose behaviour we want to change. They need not be the people who behave in an 'unwanted' way. For example, young men having fun at the waterside are the risk group for drowning and are therefore one important target group in an anti-drowning programme. But we must think about the individuals and/or organisations whose activities help the problem to persist or exacerbate it, or who interact with the target group. Also, there may be groups or organisations who have the necessary resources to help realise the programme. Doing it solo may be tempting, but partnerships can achieve more. These groups are called *stakeholders*. For example, the local city or county government is a significant stakeholder in revamping a city neighbourhood. In some cases, the boundaries between target groups and stakeholders are blurred and they may also overlap. Therefore, it may be helpful to use the term 'actor' generally for the people who are directly or indirectly involved in the planned changes, who act in our territory. Placing them in rigid boxes of target groups and stakeholders may sometimes be misleading.

There is no one fool-proof rule in dividing the relevant actors. One option is to distinguish only one or two target groups in a very detailed way. Divisions into potential groups are found when defining the problem and describing the problematic practice. In getting to know the target audience, statistics, surveys, reports by authorities or independent organisations and media publications are usually used. In addition, we strongly urge getting acquainted with everyday life in the environment in which the people live, i.e., go into the 'field'. The best way is to live among the studied people in order to have an immediate experience of their life. However, this is rarely possible. Instead, short-term observations and conversations can be used, as well as small experiments (e.g., making control purchases to see how the staff of a shop are fulfilling their obligations to inform customers or not to sell alcoholic drinks to minors).

Naturally, not all activities related to social problems are accessible to an outsider. For example, it is quite impossible to infiltrate 'communities' of school bullies or their victims. Sometimes a careful walk through the surroundings or observing relevant interactions in social networks can offer valuable insight into the details of everyday life.

Target groups usually have some common key features that are relevant to the programme. Socio-demographic characteristics are usually the first port of call, but they rarely correspond well with the boundaries of problematic practices. The Danish social researcher Bente Halkier (in press) proposes a practice-based approach in communicating risk, health and other complicated themes to non-expert audiences. Defining the social change programme's target groups in relation to their habits or actions is more fruitful for our purposes.

In addition, *power relations* and *interactions* among practitioners (e.g., who influences whom) are vital, because performances are often collective actions. In this context a very brief excursion into the notion of a 'community of practice' is necessary. Etienne Wenger (1998) has theorised about informal communities of practice that people form as they pursue shared enterprises over time. The concept has been criticised because of its implications of clear boundaries, membership, coherence and identity. Yet if we treat these communities as loose and open-ended, and don't over-emphasise the joint enterprise and sharedness, this concept may be useful. But although this term is widely applied in various professions and fields of social science, we would caution against using it to describe dispersed carriers of practices. Young men partying at a lakeside may form a community of practice, because they do things together and share a repertoire. Yet people who should eat 'five a day' (everyone), as the British National Health Service (n.d.) recommends, are not a community of practice, because that would stretch the term so far as to make it almost meaningless.

But even if we refrain from referring to a community, it may be worthwhile to analyse the 'careers' of practitioners, i.e., who is a newcomer, who is an expert, who is a regular and who is not. This usually reveals power relations. In the school bullying prevention programme referred to above, neither the bullies nor their fans, but the passive witnesses/bystanders appeared to be the key target group, whose behaviour orchestrated the whole bullying practice: if they had some guidance and encouragement to stop being a silent, yet approving public, the violence would decrease.

When the key actors are delineated, they need to be positioned in relation to the aims of the programme. This can be done in different ways. One of the most widespread is the hierarchy of effects or deficit model (Halkier, in press), which defines the target group according to the skill, knowledge or 'right attitude' that they lack. Thus programmes aim to fill gaps to make people behave in desired ways. This approach focuses on single individuals by extracting them from the network of social relations and the socio-material conditions. In Chapter 2 we introduced the Giddensian term *agency*, which encompasses the ability of an actor to observe, modify or create rules, as well as to utilise resources. Habits are not always a result of intended actions, but have become fixed in the interaction of various surrounding factors. Skills, knowledge and resources of individuals should certainly be considered when designing a programme, but so should the factors that create habits and constraints: efforts should be made to understand the depth and breadth of the actual space of opportunities and freedom of choice of different actors.

Figure 3.11 provides scales[2] which segment the key actors – target groups or stakeholders – according to their agency in relation to the planned change, based on whether a particular group has *extensive* or *limited capacity and freedom* for a change in existing habits in terms of skills, knowledge, material resources, authority etc. (vertical dimension). The second dimension forecasts how profoundly the change will affect the existing practices of the actor (horizontal dimension). On the basis of this (seemingly rather easy, yet actually quite demanding) charting exercise a decision – even if only preliminary – can be made as to how *amenable* to change the given actor and the practice are. Potential levels of resistance can be predicted in this way. These dimensions that characterise key actors should not be treated as cognitive states of mind of people, but as (shifting) positions the actors enter into vis-a-vis various socio-material affordances in the territory. This exercise can also be a planning tool when there is not much known about the target groups and stakeholders. Visualisation is also important.

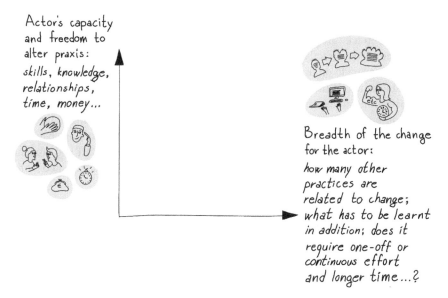

Figure 3.11   Axes of analysing and mapping key actors of the programme

2   A similar matrix is used in public relations to segment stakeholders. For example, the 'power/influence' and 'interest' matrix that was published in the late 1980s (Gardner, Rachlin and Sweeny, 1986) is still popular. In using the matrix in Figure 3.11, we have considered that actors' choices and opportunities are constrained by social structure. To put it simply, our model is less voluntary, as explained in Chapter 2 above.

Think, stretch and sketch
Think about your latest project. Who were the key actors (target groups, stakeholders and beneficiaries) in this project? Map them using the axes given in Figure 3.11.

Analysing the following microlevel case provides an illustration. Let's imagine that we want to improve food selection in the canteen of university X and introduce organic food there. The objective is to offer three organic meals in addition to ordinary meals during breakfast and lunch. The key actors involved are the manager and employees of the canteen (the chef and chef's assistants), the supplier of foodstuffs and the clients of the canteen: students and staff of the university, as well as the administration of the university, who negotiate contracts with the operators of the canteen.

In this case – and in other similar cases – we cannot distinguish between the target group and stakeholder group: the manager, chef and chef's assistants represent them both. We want to modify their food-preparation practices. The selection of food in the canteen and the prospects for other pro-environmental actions of the university depend on their responsiveness.

The capacity of the university administration to contribute is high, but specific. The operator of the canteen is selected in an open bid. Its conditions and the ensuing contracts are significant coordinating agents. Thus the administration cannot intervene directly in the management of the canteen: they cannot issue an order to provide organic food. Yet ways to liaise with the administration need to be established. If the experiment is successful and the clients are satisfied, the administration can revise the conditions for the next bid and introduce an organic food requirement. Thus their capacity is rather strong, in general, although rather symbolic. The administration is potentially rather amenable to this change because it does not take much special effort from them, and can lead to staff and student satisfaction (especially when the identity of the university is associated with 'green' values).

The manager of the canteen is a critical player in the programme. Her capacity is high, but constrained: she may have goodwill and personal preferences, but she still has to take into account the potentially higher price and limited availability of organic foodstuffs, as well as the skills of the chef to handle them. The breadth of change for the manager certainly depends on how well these issues are tackled. Thus the canteen employees may need assistance in solving daily practical problems to make them more responsive. For example, financial calculations, supply network contacts, recipes and training of the cooks need to be organised. While ordinary foodstuffs often come prepared (e.g., frozen or chopped), organic food may require extra work. Should the chef be compensated financially? Or are there other ways to motivate?

The next important stakeholder group is the chef and her assistants. Their capacity is more limited still, because the decision is made by the manager, but eventually the success of the project depends very much on how quickly the chef learns new recipes and methods and how open-mindedly she navigates the unexpected: what may come up while working with organic food. Thus, the capacity of the chef is almost as extensive – although different in nature – than the manager's. The chef's amenability to change may hinge on the financial resources to compensate the extra effort. If they are not available, other ways to offer solutions to the problems she faces may be needed. The flexibility of the kitchen staff depends very much on their relationships with the manager and clients, as well as personal curiosity and learning skills. The last, but definitely not least important, target group is the clients of the canteen. Their capability is defined mainly in terms of money (are they able to pay higher prices?), taste (do they like the new food?) and curiosity (new choices), as well as green and healthy values. The weight of the latter can easily be overestimated. If the organic food proves to be considerably pricier, the low-income students may have to abandon their pro-environment ideals. In comparison with the personnel of the canteen, their capability is rather restricted. Their amenability is higher because the change does not require much effort from them.

In general, the capability of target group members is prescribed by their social relations and position and can be seen as relatively stable. The position in terms of resistance-amenability is more dynamic and dependent on the terms of the programme. The programme team has to assess their own resources critically because, in trying to keep the target/stakeholder groups motivated, the programme initiators may run out of time, energy and enthusiasm. In the organic food example, there are many tasks to be fulfilled: communication with officials, filling in bureaucratic documents, co-operation with suppliers of foodstuffs, and persuading and supporting the chef.

Research has shown that too much flexibility in satisfying all suppliers and clients may be dangerous to the programme itself. For example, an ethnographic study was conducted with two eco-food supply networks that transported foodstuffs from farms to urban clients. Only one network survived, the one that was more rigid in its business procedures, for example in taking orders from customers. The more flexible network ran into difficulty and terminated, because the whole effort was too time- and energy-consuming for the originator (Ristkok, 2014). Therefore, in the case of potentially resistant and impervious target groups, we encourage realistically accounting for the time and energy their involvement takes. Short-term endeavours are usually manageable. However, the critical question is how quickly the key actors embrace the new ways of doing something and how long external support is needed.

We suggest deliberately taking breaks to analyse the ongoing process. It is wise to divide the project into phases in terms of time (days, weeks, months …) and to try to evaluate input, in terms of time and effort. The key actors' development has to be assessed: will the new practices become self-sustainable or will pervasive support and maintenance be needed for a longer term? The relationship between the initiators' invested time and effort and the increase in stakeholders' initiative is very rarely linear (see Figure 3.12). It makes sense to draw a curve in a free-

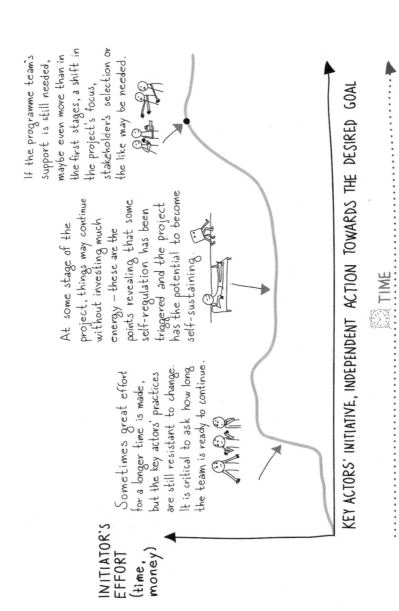

INITIATOR'S
EFFORT
(time,
money)

Sometimes great effort for a longer time is made, but the key actors' practices are still resistant to change. It is critical to ask how long the team is ready to continue.

At some stage of the project, things may continue without investing much energy — these are the points revealing that some self-regulation has been triggered and the project has the potential to become self-sustaining.

If the programme team's support is still needed, maybe even more than in the first stages, a shift in the project's focus, stakeholder's selection or the like may be needed.

KEY ACTORS' INITIATIVE, INDEPENDENT ACTION TOWARDS THE DESIRED GOAL

TIME

Figure 3.12   Analysis of the ratio of time, energy and other investments and the results in terms of change

form drawing and use it as a tool in making decisions about how to continue the project. This is one way of dealing with complexity and open situations, because it is impossible to give one fool-proof recipe for making such calculations. The initiators themselves are not outsiders, but embedded in the process. How much are they ready to invest in the project? After a test period an evaluation should definitely occur, comparing the feedback of key actors with the first impressions of programme makers. On the basis of that data, future decisions can be made.

3.5 Coalition building

Forming a coalition of stakeholders leads to achieving objectives that stakeholder organisations alone are not capable of. The effectiveness of the outcome of co-operation should be the reason for investing time and effort in the coalition in the first place. The idea of building a coalition looks simple on paper. However, it differs in the behaviour-change and practice-based approaches.

In the practice-oriented approach the difference between stakeholders and target groups is not always clear, as in order to change somebody's practices the key may lie in changing others' practices. For example, the choices of food by the customers of a canteen are up to those who compose the menu. In addressing individuals' eating habits, customers are usually treated as a target group and the canteen as a stakeholder, but in the practice-oriented view the canteen's organisation can also be approached as a target group and the customers can be seen as stakeholders, as they support the new menu and, by doing so, facilitate relevant action by the management of the canteen. In order to reduce the confusion of differentiation between stakeholders and target groups, it is convenient to use the concept of *actors* and map their ways of relating and positioning (resources and ability to change the order of things; see Figure 3.13).

Despite the advantages of actors' mutual networking, in which they bring their knowledge, resources and contacts into the programme, the coalition may not be successful in accomplishing its aims. This may happen because the actors who may want to change somebody else's ways of acting may not have direct access to change mechanisms and, *vice versa*, those who can actually address the relevant practices and their carriers may not be interested in revising their own routines. Usually coalitions are based on actors all supporting the same cause; for example, partnerships against unhealthy habits are formed of individuals and organisations who want to establish healthy diets. But unwanted habits (unhealthy eating) or desired habits (healthy eating) may rely on various conditions: taste, nutritional value etc. For example, the habit of unhealthy eating may be based on saving time: healthy meals (shopping, preparing and cooking) take time and may be sacrificed for other needs. Instructions by scientists, school programmes and corporate money that are included in social marketing campaigns and the availability of healthy foodstuffs may not work here, as the busy lifestyles of families with children and the constraints that ensue are not addressed.

Coalition building demands a lot of time and resources from its participants. Guidebooks of coalition building suggest regular coalition meetings, preparation of monthly newsletters, the formation of shared information systems etc. However, the actors whose actions have the biggest impact on relevant practices may not have a strategic interest in a particular coalition. The world is complex and organisations have to choose between many alternative missions, alongside their central mission. They cannot fulfil all of them. However, the fact that a big corporation has no motivation to spend the energy of its corporate social responsibility office on framing values, establishing goals, involvement in a jumble of endless coordination and communication with another 'world improving' coalition does not mean that the resources of the corporation are totally unavailable for the cause. For most organisations a coalition means distraction from its central aims and a mess of power relations. It must be made easier for them, i.e., a coalition has to be habitable.

The management of a coalition is usually oriented to the empowerment of a leading organisation or its particular programme. This assumes that the participants in the coalition all look in one direction and channel their support into a one-dimensional action. But the abstract goals of the coalition, e.g., to diminish poverty, and their implementation may not touch on conditions that directly influence practice change. Therefore, attempts to gather wide communities under the umbrella of a coalition may not guarantee deep and sustainable changes.

In building a successful coalition, the guidebook of the Western Organization of Resource Councils (2010) encourages defining the main goals and self-interests of partner organisations. The coalition can increase its potential to change social structures by defining whose resources and regulations empower unwanted practices or can empower desired practices.

Think and stretch

In the framework of a nationwide programme aiming to reduce sugar consumption among toddlers, the idea of launching a special kids' bottled water brand was put on the table in a co-creation event with toddlers. As a project manager, you have to create a coalition to discuss the realisation of this idea. Which partners would you invite to the coalition and why (see Figure 3.13)?

The guidebook of Western Organization of Resource Councils (2010) says that a coalition is like a chain, whose strength is measured not by its length, but by its weakest link. Thus the following steps may be envisaged in mapping a coalition around a problematic practice:

- Checking out which group is the weakest link in the practice change programme.
- Building the coalition around its triggers: ones that can empower wanted practices and those that can impede unwanted ones.

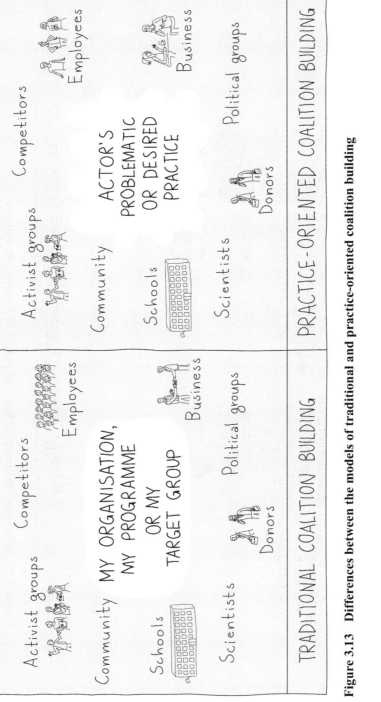

Figure 3.13 Differences between the models of traditional and practice-oriented coalition building

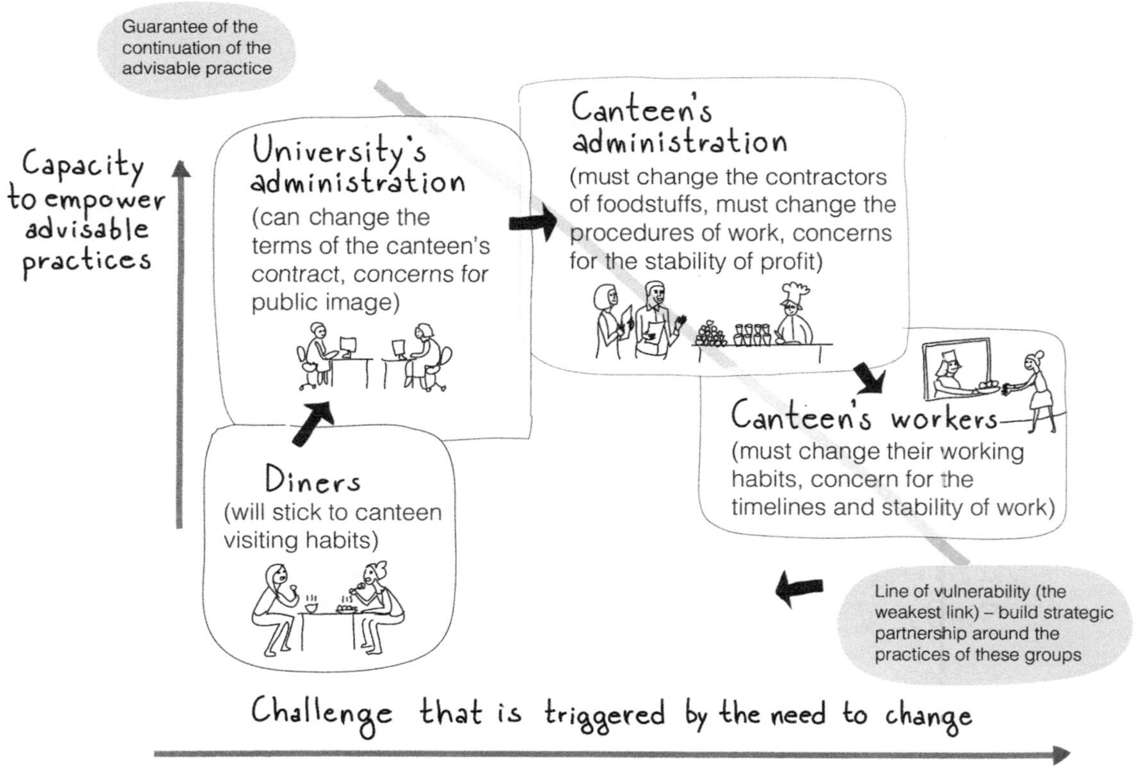

Figure 3.14 Key actors in changing the food supply of a university canteen

- Inviting partners on board that are not just involved in problematic practice, but can also apply resources or change rules.
- Using and strengthening existing relations instead of creating new ones: this increases complexity.
- Checking whether the list of triggers is complete.
- Inviting the partners behind these triggers into your coalition.
- If the coalition does not cover the needs of the mapping, there may be a weak link in the chain and the coalition will not be able to activate a transformation in practices.

As possible partners may not share common values and possess the will to achieve them, how can power relations be built? Without agreement on power it is hard to assign any duties. In the practice-oriented approach, wide coalitions with shared power relations are not effective. A typology of partners can be a handy tool (see Figure 3.14):

1. *Knowledge groups* are those who can analyse the roots of the problematic practice or the lack of the desired one. These may be anthropologists, ethnographers, sociologists and activists or enterprises with grass-roots knowledge. Possible ways to involve them may be brainstorming to analyse the triggers of the practice and plan the roads to change, visiting them at scientific conferences and community gatherings, and everyday work in grass-roots organisations. It is always advisable to gain personal experience by stepping into practitioners' shoes.
2. *Pragmatic groups* are groups who can change the regulations (authorities) or modify the resources (authorities and business firms) that the advisable practices depend on. They will not take part in all coalition gatherings, so they should not be pressured. Their interests should be identified: can they improve profits, public image or influence? Can they safeguard their future against insecurities of competition? This group does not need to be fully involved in the intricate knowledge building about the roots and aims of the programme, as long as it supports the general aims of action.
3. *Ideological coalition* groups can actually profit from joint planning and are interested in being involved in management. These are usually citizens' organisations that are powerless when unaware of each other's actions. Engaging them in ordinary coalition building – dissemination of information and assessment of progress – may be very fruitful, while avoiding pointless networking. A weak partner can weaken the network.
4. *Innovation groups* can envision the desired practice. Is there room for innovation? Perhaps the change in practice requires regulations or resources that the present organisations lack. Seeking a new partner or creating one are ideas to consider.

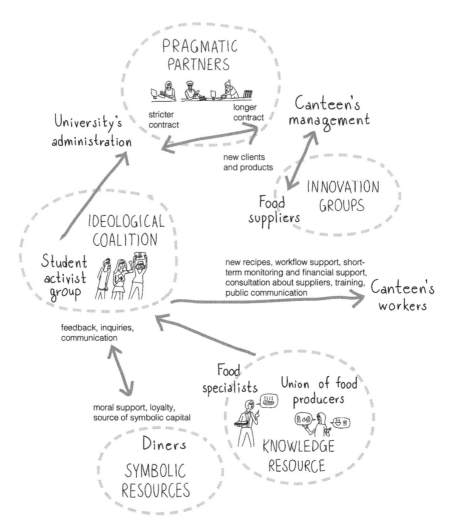

Figure 3.15 Network to change the food policy of a university's canteen

Although a coalition does not require networking between all members, it still requires management. The organisation forming the coalition should do some self-reflection first: what are the abilities of our organisation? What languages do we speak? What do we look like? What are our professional practices? The tasks of the parts of the coalition that are able and willing to convene under the same umbrella of mission and values should be divided according to these questions (Bourdieu, 1989). There may be members of the coalition who can negotiate with business leaders and politicians, some that can easily find a common language with specialists on social problems, some that are good at administration and some who are capable of protesting in the streets. This means sharing tasks and business relations according to strengths and not forcing the members of organisations to become who they are not.

3.6 Opportunities and constraints of the strategic approach

Choosing a strategy and tactics, and finding a good balance between analysis and action are challenging tasks. Below we sum up the main points of this chapter by using one hypothetical case.

The protagonist is a leader of a group of environmental activists. Most members of the group were rather radical eco-activists in their youth, so the local community is wary of their actions. Over the years the group has become more moderate and does not strive to change the whole world in one fight, but settles for smaller step-by-step developments. The objective for next year is to decrease usage of cars in a 4 km^2 neighbourhood of nearly 4,000 inhabitants, called 'Green Meadow'.

In 'translating' the problem into everyday behaviour patterns (see section 3.1 above), the group has found out that, in addition to commuting to offices and schools, a sizeable number of the evening and weekend car trips are made to a local shopping centre. Commuting routes vary significantly and offering solutions to all of them would be too complicated a task. So the team has decided to start with a manageable chunk and has selected a strategy to substitute the current 'drive-to-shop' with 'bike-to-shop' or 'walk-to-shop' practices (see section 3.3 above).

In order to estimate the chosen strategy and start designing tactics, an analysis of the project's territory and its socio-material network is needed (see section 3.2 above).

The distance between the shop and the residential district, the condition of streets and roads, weather, and the social benefits of bicycling and walking form the nodes of the socio-material network. In addition, attention must be paid to safety (theft of bikes), the places/shelters to park bicycles in residential and office areas, the possibility of taking a shower at offices after a bike ride, general traffic safety etc.

It is wise to start with smaller well-known units (places, organisations, subgroups etc.), collect similar information about other units, and then generalise. There is no one correct path, but many possible methods of conducting a socio-material network analysis: comparative tables, area maps and visualisations of each area.

Table 3.2 gives an example of how to make the pro-bicycling socio-material network visible (ways to obtain information are given in brackets).

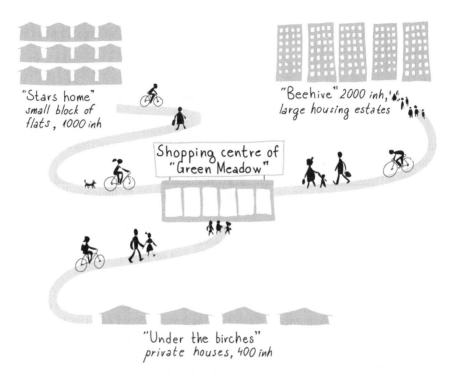

Figure 3.16   The imagined map of the 'Green Meadow' neighbourhood, the territory in the programme to reduce car use

From this grid possible aims of the (communication) project emerge quite clearly: in order to reinforce 'greener' everyday mobility practices, communication and project management should first consider the infrastructural conditions.

The slogan 'Walk or cycle to your everyday shopping' would work best with residents in the first area and would be least effective with the residents in the third area, because the distance to walk and carry shopping bags is rather long. Also, there are material obstacles to bicycling (no shelters to safely park bikes). Depending on the resources, there may be various ways to build the social change programme (see Table 3.2).

Too narrow an approach (e.g., by launching a 'pure' communication campaign with the above slogan) may attract only a small number of inhabitants, for whom it is relatively convenient (safe and good roads, and place to keep bicycles). But how long can they keep it up if the vast majority of inhabitants still drive? This option might be the easiest (no additional resources and message 'directly' to the end-users), but also the most short-lived intervention.

Another way is to focus communication on the local authorities (especially before elections) with the aim of repairing local roads and organising some kind of financially acceptable collective solution for equipping buildings with bike

Table 3.2   Sample table for analysing the pro-bicycling socio-material network

	First area, called 'stars home' Recently built smaller blocks of flats for young middle-class families	Second area, called 'under the birches' Private houses, older inhabitants, 'older' than two other areas	Third area, called 'beehive' Big housing estates, heterogeneous inhabitant profile (young singles and couples, big families …)	Tactical programme options
Approx. number of inhabitants (source: local government)	1,000	400	2,000	The population densities in different areas suggest that a change would affect more people when initiated in the third area.
Average distance between the shopping centre and the residential areas (source: planning documents, real estate advertising, own measurements)	300m	500m	1,000m	Some areas closer, but in general the distance is suitable for bicycling; some areas also suitable for walking to the shopping centre. Bicycling as a more universal suggestion is better to include at the centre of the action plan; walking is an alternative mainly in the first area.
Conditions of roads: lighting, road cover (observation)	two roads in bad condition (missing lighting)	six roads in bad condition (cover, lighting)	three roads in bad condition (cover)	Bicycling needs to be safe. Improvement in condition of 11 roads to support bicycling/ walking. This makes the local authorities key stakeholders (see the next stakeholder and target group analysis matrix).
Traffic density in peak hours (expert opinion, counting/observation)	high	medium	medium	The traffic density needs to be lowered in the first area. One option is to launch a step-by-step programme, motivating the first area residents' mobilisation (see the stakeholders' and target group's analysis matrix).
Places to keep bicycles in the residential areas (sources: observation, survey of administrators of the block houses)	Exist near 40% of houses	Exist near 90% of houses	Exist near 10% of houses	Places to keep bicycles especially critical in the third area. Thus, in parallel with the road improvement campaign, a community programme has to be initiated aimed at creating bicycle shelters and parking spaces near houses.

shelters. The drawback of this option is too long a waiting time for the results to emerge.

A third way – our proposal – is to start a multi-dimensional social change programme that involves both meanings and physical environments. Generally, it is wiser to begin with a smaller area with a holistic change programme than to conduct a narrowly focused campaign in a large area, whose outcomes may be short-term, providing no success story to draw upon in future initiatives of the team.

To make final decisions key actor analysis plays a major role. We suggest using visualisation, for example in the form of a matrix. The capabilities of the inhabitants in the three areas are not equal. The residents of the 'star house' district (first area) are most qualified: they are young (thus physically more fit), have the shortest distance to go, and have two options (walking or cycling). Thus their responsiveness to change should be the highest. But their family lifestyle and weekly rhythms need to be explored before making final judgements. Do they go shopping once a week and buy in bulk? In this case carrying bags would still be a problem and we need to persuade them to shop more frequently and buy fewer things at a time. This suggestion may have strengths (buying only things one really needs, and less impulse and just-in-case purchases), but that could interfere with many other practices that make up families' weekly routines. Thus observations and perhaps a quick survey (questionnaires in mailboxes of selected houses) about shopping frequencies are prudent.

The inhabitants of the third area are probably the least responsive as they face the most obstacles. To motivate them, communication with local authorities to make road repairs and arrange bicycle parking is needed. This, in turn, generates the need for coalition building (see section 3.5) to negotiate with the local government, which may not be very enthusiastic about dealing with the former 'eco-radicals'. Thus the mapping of potential allies is needed. Perhaps pro-environment parents in the local school council are good partners (being part of the electorate).

A model that works smoothly in smaller test sites may not function as well in larger and more complex contexts. There may be many reasons for that: (1) the social capital of community (e.g., if there is a lawyer among the inhabitants, she may do the necessary paperwork on a voluntary basis, but in a bigger programme extra cost is incurred); (2) social norms (e.g., even though I am not 'green', I will participate in order to maintain good rapport with my neighbours); and (3) extra gains (e.g., establishing co-operation with neighbours increases neighbourhood safety). In a larger site, where relations between people are more formal, volunteer work and social norms may not be the main pillars of the programme and extra expenses and efforts need to be invested to accomplish similar results.

Thus when selecting the approach, one should lay the foundation for future transferability and scalability of solutions.

3.7 Summary

This chapter has encouraged readers to acknowledge the complexity and 'wickedness' of social problems, i.e., making sense of open-ended situations, while demarcating a territory – even if temporary – where one can make a difference. Problem framings, in the language of social practices, are a crucial point of departure, i.e., social issues should be translated from statistical and expert phrasings of law, medicine etc. into the language of everyday life. What are people doing in a harmful or irresponsible manner today and why? How can this be re-crafted? For this analysis, the concept of a socio-material network (of environments, things, people and their interactions) is utilised: a web of different players and phenomena, where the most meaningful units form nodes. Social practices can be seen as embedded in this socio-material network. The four-element model of practices – meanings, things/material environments, skills and social interaction as an integrative dynamic within and between practices – provides a framework in the programme background research phase. Along this line of thinking, the available programme objective formulations are: creating new practices, and modifying, substituting or disrupting existing practices. Lower-density compound practices – less tightly coordinated bundles of activities – may be more responsive to new practice creation, whereas firmly organised practices could be (though only in extreme cases) completely disrupted in the course of achieving some sort of transition.

The traditional division between target groups and stakeholders is complemented by a more flexible 'key actor' concept, as the boundary between target groups and stakeholders may be blurry and they may even switch roles along the way. Actor capability and potential breadth of change mapping is meant to shed light on who should potentially be involved and how. Coalition building is a challenging process with no room for illusions, since actors in different fields (the market, policy-making or civil society) have different rationales and mechanisms of activity. Yet taking the desired practices as departure points – i.e., which organisations can trigger and empower the new or modified practices – if done meaningfully, can lead to breakthroughs and encourage pragmatic co-operation. Potential coalition partners can be explored as knowledge, innovation or pragmatic groups, or they can help to form an ideological coalition.

These analytic exercises and territory 'reconnaissance' provide a basis for selecting strategic courses of action for concrete programme design and implementation.

Further reading

Theoretical approaches and reports

Phillips, L.J. (2011). *The promise of dialogue*. Amsterdam, The Netherlands: John Benjamins Publishing.
Shove, E., Pantzar, M. and Watson, M. (2012). *The dynamics of social practice. Everyday life and how it changes*. London, England: Sage.
Spurling, N., McMeekin, A., Shove, E., Southerton, D. and Welch, D. (2013). Interventions in practice: Re-framing policy approaches to consumer behaviour. Sustainable Practices Research Group Report. Retrieved from http://www.sprg.ac.uk/uploads/sprg-report-sept-2013.pdf

Web tools that help to organise ideas visually

Evaluation Toolbox (n.d.). Problem tree / Solution tree analysis. Retrieved from http://evaluationtoolbox.net.au/index.php?option=com_content&view=article&id=28&Itemid=134
Worksheet Works (n.d.). Graphic organizers. Retrieved from http://www.worksheetworks.com/miscellanea/graphic-organizers.html

Policy documents – some examples of how to start a search

European Commission (n.d.). The policies. Retrieved from http://ec.europa.eu/policies/index_en.htm
European Environment Agency (n.d.). Environmental policy document catalogue. Retrieved from http://www.eea.europa.eu/policy-documents#c5=all&c0=10&b_start=0
World Health Organization (n.d.). Policy documents. Retrieved from http://www.who.int/hrh/documents/policy/en/

Chapter 4

Designing an effective and sustainable programme

This chapter elaborates on various activities and methods of intervention structured according to the main practice element – meanings, things/environments or skills – they address. Although such a division is bound to be somewhat arbitrary and simplified, its objective is to provide for systematic thinking in programme design. Each section places programme building blocks in a theoretical framework, which guides the reader in making choices among them and designing cohesive activities (together with coalition partners) that in one way or another affect all practice components. Towards the end of the chapter, a brief overview of social innovation as a new integrative concept is provided. The chapter ends with some down-to-earth advice on implementation, without going into tactical or operational detail.

4.1 Elements of the design of a change programme

As stressed above, the success of a programme is determined by how *comprehensively* the target social problem can be dealt with at the level of *everyday life*. A programme should be designed so that it affects all elements of a practice: meanings, physical environment, competences and social interaction, the 'glue' between them. Even though such a holistic endeavour does not guarantee durable practice change, it is still much closer to that than one-off campaigns addressing only one practice element. We suggest using a simple four-element model (see Figure 4.1). This can be done via a free-form drawing, which combines and relates all important constituents of the programme. This reveals which elements are weakly covered. It is essential to address *skills* and *competences* when we want to change social practices, because they appear in the form of individual enactments. In order to succeed, one has to possess relevant practical (embodied) know-how. New *competences* are acquired through hands-on training (the main tool for transferring practical consciousness-based movements) or education (acknowledged, rationalised actions based on discursive consciousness). *Meanings* refer to the understandings, values and ideologies that the programme wants to promote. Actors' meanings are usually heterogeneous and dispersed, and the task of the programme maker is to find the symbols and messages that link with the meanings that circulate among the key actors and re-shape, focus or re-locate them in order to make them more supportive of the change. Social advertising works on meanings, but it does not alter the physical environment. When launching an advertising campaign, actors are required to muddle through by themselves if they get entangled in (micro-)problems that stem from the *physical environment*. *Material things*, *regulations*, *technologies* etc., which make up the physical environment, are important building blocks of the social change programme. It may be tempting to regard regulations and infrastructure as too difficult to deal with and best left untouched. Here we suggest (a) starting with minor changes in the physical environment (re-designing room interiors, providing direction signs, creating spaces that are conducive to discussion etc.), (b) creating smaller test sites, and (c) seeking coalition partners who are or might become interested in similar legislation or infrastructure improvement. It is worthwhile to involve both beneficiaries and coalition partners before fleshing out creative solutions. Instead of the somewhat over-used focus group method, one should consider setting up co-creation workshops or free discussions with other professionals who are faced with similar projects (not necessarily in the same field or territory).

Additional action plans and timetables can be devised according to types of activities, (communication) channels etc., but target practice elements have to be returned to on a regular basis to double-check against distortions (information without material support etc.).

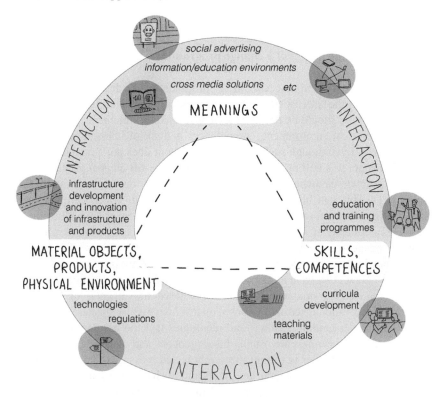

Figure 4.1   Elements of social change programme design

The two other factors to consider in programme management are resources and time-lines (often interrelated). Usually programmes are divided into phases, and resources are allocated to each phase. If the overall aim is to ensure results' *sustainability over time*, this rarely can be achieved by relying on the scant project budget of one organisation alone. This brings us back to the need for coalition building. The new normality, i.e., a practice that encompasses a significant number of people, probably cannot be reached in a week, a month or maybe even years. Thus adapting and *redesigning* a programme is inevitable if we want to come to terms with the complexity of everyday life. This shows the need to provide for certain stages or reflection pauses in the process to take stock of the current situation and re-design the programme accordingly. Looking back helps to stay determined. What were the impacts of previous interventions? Which modifications had to be made in earlier programmes and why? How was the initiators' everyday life re-crafted? In its abstract, theoretical form, a comprehensive approach to a social change programme appears to be complicated. However, when performing a specific task, it is a logical way to address a problem.

In sections 4.2, 4.3 and 4.4 of this chapter we introduce the main tools of programme making, categorised by the elements of practice. Social interaction as the integrating dynamic is a common thread that runs all through the design process, and therefore we dedicate no special section to that.

4.2 Material objects, products and environment

Any social change is embedded in the material environment in which people work, study and play. The availability of goods, services and information, mobility opportunities and communication devices significantly affect our everyday practices and our understanding of what is normal and desirable.

4.2.1 Infrastructure and built environment

The functioning of infrastructure and the built environment in shaping social practices cannot be underestimated. According to Geels (2005), a researcher of socio-technical transitions, all kinds of infrastructures and material items, along with the regulatory environment, form the basis of stabilisation of socio-technical systems,[1] as mutual role commitments between individuals are invested in these

---

1 *Socio-technical system* is, according to Geels (2004), a term for innovation systems that includes both the supply side (innovations) and the demand side (user environment). Contrary to his predecessors, Frank Geels stresses that the development of innovative knowledge should be linked to the functionality and user side, impacts and societal transformations. Our use of a similar concept, *socio-material network*, differs from Geels's concept by focusing centrally on 'user experience' and its connectedness to different systems of innovation.

components. The introduction of new skills and attributing new meanings are usually tied to the creation of a relevant material environment.

For example, the skills and meanings of a shopping practice are locked into the materiality of the socio-technical system of the retail sector. The repetitive enactment of shopping determines the infrastructure of retailing as a preordained material environment for shopping.

Table 4.1 shows that materiality is linked to tightly coordinated sales, display and marketing practices of high density. If the social practice of shopping, for example, is to be shifted in a more ecological direction, a question emerges: is it wiser to change the existing material order of the practice or to provide the

Table 4.1   The connectedness of materiality in the socio-technical system of the retail sector

Skills and meanings	The way infrastructure, artefacts and regulations of retailing are embodied in relevant skills and meanings
skills to orientate on the landscape of shopping, to look for the shopping spots in unfamiliar locations	*artefacts:* road signs, appearance of buildings *infrastructure:* the way social services are combined in public places *regulations:* the code of marketing symbols
skills to follow shopping rules	*artefacts:* room design, product price tags, room signs, shopping carts, personnel *infrastructure:* the way the pathway between the entrance and cashier is built up, social addressing in the store *regulations:* paying and queuing, patterns of conduct of other visitors
the skills to choose products	*artefacts:* product information on packaging, shelves *infrastructure:* product assortment, relations with producers *regulations:* what to consider a product, regulations about packaging, fashion
(symbolic) meanings of shopping, products	*artefacts:* the appearance of products and shopping site *infrastructure:* product assortment (market, boutique or coffee shop?), convenience of car parks, space design *regulations:* marketing regulations (e.g., about alcohol), collective rituals of buying, discounts and special offers

consumer with a new one? Retailing is strongly stabilised through participants' different investments in infrastructure, material items and regulations. This impedes innovations in the regime other than incremental ones: tiny changes that raise the density of practice and may therefore also repel the consumer.

Effecting radical changes in stabilised socio-technical systems does not depend solely on radical planning. According to Frank Geels (2005), there is a need for playfulness and blind chance. In order to prompt an alternative regime, small niches of innovation need to be created that can function as incubation sites. As a result, new socio-material networks can be built based not on rational planning, but on diffuse and often irrational trajectories of thinking that can aggregate unexpected combinations of technology, user preferences, regulations, infrastructure and symbolic meanings.

For example, in order to provide consumers with organic food, a solution can be found through niching. The change will not start with the success of the niche network, but of competing niches that can together disrupt the seamless web of a ruling socio-technical regime. The participants in these networks need to accept the investment in new artefacts, infrastructures and rules as a beneficial choice. Each new participant in this alternative web contributes to its stabilisation by linking new functional elements together.

At present organic alternatives to ordinary retailing – urban gardening, food networks, eco-shops, e-shops and distribution in existing supermarkets – usually operate as incremental innovations that do not challenge the ruling regime. In order to mainstream an organic shopping regime, an infrastructure is needed that is capable of competing with the seemingly inevitable dominant regime.

Think and stretch

What types of individuals can eco-shops with different locations recruit? Which location has the greatest potential to attract visitors with no particular environmental affiliations?

… a shopping centre, among fashion boutiques

… a suburban residential district (no parking lot)

… a large pharmacy

… a separate section in an ordinary supermarket

Infrastructures' organisational features guarantee interconnections between the structural elements of society. They may take different forms, e.g., virtual (information systems) or physical (shops and roads). Usually they co-exist and intermingle. Infrastructures and environments are also always socio-material, not just physical, because they cannot be configured in a random, but only in a socio-culturally meaningful way. For example, a significant part of physical infrastructure is formed by the hours and days when the facility is open (e.g., on national holidays), which may change the way the material framework is used. Social meanings unite the elements of a socio-material environment into a unique infrastructure complex. In programme design, choices have to be made about whether to create new infrastructure that triggers new practices, or to change the existing infrastructure to support the integrity of new practices. For example, shopping is a relatively dense and complex practice; it involves most spheres of life. It is easier to build a relevant infrastructure by combining elements that are already familiar to consumers. Completely new infrastructures can be useful if new practices completely replace old ones (e.g., in consumers' daily schedules) or the new practice is less dense (less competition for consumers' time). Frequent and coherent practices demand more compatibility with an existing material environment than non-recurrent ones do. For example, a person is more willing to take his old furniture than his more ordinary everyday waste to a distant reclamation centre. However, adoption of a performance is easier if it follows elements of practice that can be re-used for other purposes.

A good example of this kind of infrastructure is Finnish Cleaning Day (in Finnish: Siivouspäivä), which relies on combining elements of existing social practices in a new way (http://siivouspaiva.com). On a day in May anyone can offer their personal second-hand items for sale in streets, parks and front-yards. The event relies on the initiatives of individuals. Each person has to clean up after himself. Cleaning Day draws on people's habits of spring-cleaning and going to flea markets. This festival turns cities and neighbourhoods into giant second-hand markets twice a year.

**Figure 4.2   Cleaning Day in Helsinki – anyone can offer their personal
                second-hand items for sale in streets, parks and front-yards**
Photo by Helen Ennok

It would be much more difficult to take part in a regional plant and seedling exchange festival, as the threshold for initiators is much higher: to exchange plants one has to be committed to long-term habits of gardening.

Think, stretch and sketch
Draw a plan of an infrastructure that supports solving the problem of public urination in city centres.

Even though material and virtual infrastructures may be tricky to finance because of very high costs and the risks involved in potential consumer-citizen response and appropriation, we nevertheless encourage thoroughly analysing and exploring the potential for changing environments in coalition with business, state and civil actors, because practice change – due to the very nature of practice composition – requires some, perhaps only slight, reconfiguration of environments and things. The next section provides greater detail in this area.

4.2.2 Products and technologies

It is difficult to separate infrastructures and environments from products, technologies and physical objects. So this section elaborates on the previous section.

Objects are components of practices, so there is no change without an alteration in how people handle artefacts, consume products, and do things within the material world. The notion of material agency refers to the power of objects and technologies to shape what people do, as well as be shaped by action 'beyond what was originally planned in the technology design phase' (Sahakian and Wilhite, 2014, p. 29). Thus it is not only people who handle objects and do things with them, it is also vice versa. Human activity is constantly changing in the interaction between humans and objects. Therefore, social change attempts need to take things seriously. Lots of communication and social marketing efforts tend to emphasise meanings only and underplay the role of materiality. Yet, there are many situations where physical objects are successfully included in campaigns. Think back to the marrow donor promoting bandages (Help! I want to save a life) (Douglas, n.d.) or recall the 2014 award-winning campaign by Nivea for sun block cream, which featured a kid-tracking mobile app and gadget (Pathak, 2014) or the designer carafe to promote tap water in London restaurants (Sahakian and Wilhite, 2014).

Examination of the existing material reality reveals how objects connect to the problem at hand. In other words, if an analysis of 'bad' practices or bundles is carried out, the material, or sometimes (information) technological configurations of things, without which the particular practices could not exist, need to be scrutinised. What are the items and objects involved? What are their particular affordances and characteristics (content, design or functionality) that constitute part of the problem? How do people use those objects and technologies? What do they physically do with them and what do they say about them?

Think and stretch

There is a well-known programme in the UK and many other countries promoting eating five portions of fruit and vegetables a day. Offer specific fruit- and vegetable-related creative ideas that intervene in the material world (not just media communication) and help support the idea (e.g., a plate that measures portions).

On the other end of the scale, there is the imagined desired 'good' practice, the new normality. Material objects and technologies are also involved here. Technological innovation and engineers' and designers' imaginations are paramount. For example, reflectors that save pedestrian lives in traffic during dark hours are products created to solve the specific problem of road safety. For the desired practice to take root, either newly created products and technologies have to be introduced, or existing ones have to be adapted to make them healthier, more sustainable and more responsible. Thousands of products are created and developed in commercial markets without a specific social problem in mind, yet each of them claims to satisfy some sort of need. In some cases, those innovations can be harnessed to help solve social problems.

Risky products as focal points in problematic practices To embed some kind of system into the very versatile world of material objects and goods, first those items that are the primary foci of the intended change, i.e., problematic or risky products that stand at the centre of certain 'vices' of the consumer society, need to be examined. Alcohol, tobacco and unhealthy food are the prime examples. From the service sector pay-day loans come to mind first. When designing a programme, it is instructive to consider whether there is a central material object category or perhaps a technology that deserves specific attention. If this exists, informing and persuading people, trying to motivate them to choose a better behaviour, will almost always not be enough. If the problem lies in the relationship between the behaviour and the material or technological items, the latter must be addressed, too. However, this is not meant to encourage short-cuts that deal only with some aspects of the object, leaving the remaining social practice (meanings, social interactions, skills and relations with other practices) intact.

There is a large variety of ways in which products and material objects can be included within a social change intervention. Some are more readily available to the programme maker, such as product-focused information campaigns, while some are not and must be dealt with at higher policy levels or by manufacturers and sellers. When such items stand at the core of a problem, it may be easier to use economic and regulatory means to curb or reform their usage. The measures include:

- regulations and financial measures: banning, sales restrictions, taxes or subsidies to reconfigure consumer access and usage of a product;
- product (and/or service) innovation (e.g., self-extinguishing cigarettes, lighter alcohol, additive free foodstuffs etc.);
- various communicative means (information dissemination and education) to encourage people to consume less or differently, especially point-of-purchase or touch-point communication that is directly tied to the product-person interface.

Neutral items that support the existence of problematic practices. It is obvious that there are not many products that can clearly be classified as detrimental in themselves. For example, from the climate change and health point of view, there are actually more and more ordinary consumer items whose consumption in aggregate is well beyond sustainability levels. Cars, washing machines and red meat, which for decades have been parts of everyday Western normality, have become problematic. Concerns do not arise from consumption of particular objects per se, but from excess. This makes interventions in contemporary 'epistolary' (as opposed to pastoral or paternalistic; see Chapter 1) states highly challenging. It is not currently realistic – at least in most Western countries – to just ban the use of cars or even restrict it, e.g., one vehicle per household. In the case of the obesity epidemic, it is impossible to pinpoint the prime 'culprit'. There are entire food production, distribution, provision, cooking, eating, sedentary work and entertainment practices whose messy and complex configurations are 'to blame'. Taking objects seriously in such situations seems impossible. Yet there are examples of programmes where concerted efforts have been made to address people's use of some key items. An oft-cited favourite of practice theory authors (see Spurling et al., 2013; Evans, McMeekin and Southerton, 2012) is the New Nordic Diet, which combines local Nordic foodstuffs, provision systems and cooking (including recipes and instructions by celebrity chefs for school meals). Another example is the so-called Danish breakthrough with child obesity reported by the BBC in November 2014. All items in the 17-point synopsis of the programme developed by paediatricians and meant to revamp obese children's lives in one way or another touched upon materiality: the ways children engage with screens (TVs, tablets), food and drink, as well as physical activities (Brabant, 2014).

New technology and the virtual world pose increasing challenges, too. For example, if the territory is financial literacy, the range of services the key audiences and actors of the programme are influenced by is vast. These include not only bank notes and coins, but also complicated non-physical financial services that are often called 'products' by banks. Even if the service and access to it are purely virtual (one can take out a pay-day loan using a laptop and sign the contract with an ID card app without the need to see a bank clerk), the technologies and environments, both software and hardware, that render it possible, require attention.

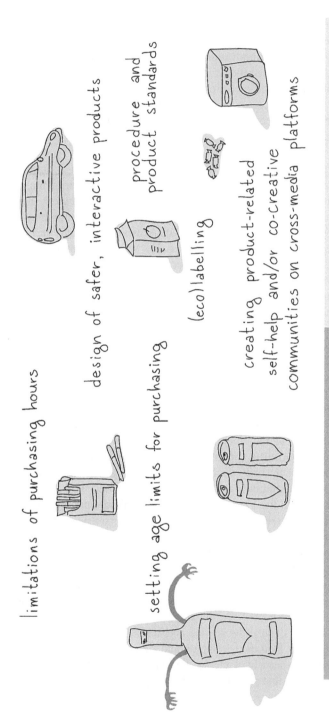

Figure 4.3   Products and the ways they can be (re-)formed

With 'neutral' products and services that can be framed as part of a problem, there is a set of measures that can be resorted to, partly overlapping with the previous category (the risky products), yet 'hard' interventions in terms of bans and regulations may be more complicated to fathom and accomplish. These measures include:

- product innovations and new technologies
- economic and regulatory means: norms and standards
- communicative and educational means (e.g., product labelling)

Here a separate area worth stressing is various new (and forgotten old) ways of use and consumption (and 'prosumption', a blurry area where consumer and producer roles overlap), such as:

- recycling and re-use
- do-it-yourself
- collaborative consumption, sharing and solidarity purchasing schemes
- fix-up and repair movements

These can be consciously employed to re-shape usage of products in new, less resource-intensive ways. Sharing has been ambitiously named as one of the 10 ideas that will change the world by *Time* magazine. The most well-known examples include the home rental AirBnB and the car-sharing Zipcar (http://www.airbnb. com; http://www.zipcar.com). In Italy the GAS movement (Gruppi Di Acuisto Solidali: collective product-purchasing and -sharing arrangements) is relatively widespread (http://www.retegas.org). Whether such initiatives will transform business models and the pillars of consumer society is yet to be seen, but they definitely modify existing practices, e.g., mobility and vacation accommodation search, and create new or revive old activities of community sharing, which have been up-scaled by the possibilities of the Internet.

Think, stretch and sketch
Design a smart home for an ailing senior citizen who lives alone. Think bold! Do not worry whether you are designing a product, service or infrastructure/environment; they are inevitably entangled.

One more category that has risen to the agenda of world-improving actions involves utilities, most notably energy. Climate change has made energy the focal point not only of technical innovation (e.g., use of renewable energy or home retrofits), but also of many intervention programmes. A rapidly emerging body of sociological research is dedicated to the 'energy and society' theme (Shove and Walker, 2014; Gram-Hanssen, 2013). The category of utilities can only very artificially be separated from the previous treatment of products in general, in that utilities do not become issues per se, but mainly in terms of resources people consume. Thus energy underlies almost all acts of consumption in contemporary Western lifestyles. We will deal with this issue separately, however, because many intervention programmes as well as research do so. Energy is an independent domain and people are constantly made more conscious of their energy consumption, with the aim of urging them to use less and use differently (e.g., to avoid peak loads on the grid). As Elizabeth Shove and Gordon Walker (2014) have pointed out, energy is not a consumer product in itself; it is an ingredient in almost all social practices that involve the consumption of goods. Thus attempts to draw peoples' attention specifically to energy are very difficult to accomplish and often have short-lived outcomes. People do not consume electricity; they clean their clothes, make coffee, go to work etc.

Here efforts involving technical innovations complemented by 'aligning' consumers to become more reflective about their energy use are numerous (e.g., Harries et al., 2013; Nyborg and Røpke, 2013). The main objective of those interventions has been to render the invisible visible through smart meters and feedback to consumers on their personal consumption, as well as 'social norm' information on neighbourhood average use etc. These efforts have had mixed results. Some confirm the efficacy of social norm information, while others do not. Energy (and water) usage are outcomes of other behaviours, which should be the targets of intervention programmes.

The basic questions summing up the above section are:

- which identifiable (consumer) objects, tangible or intangible (e.g., cars, food or pay-day loans) are involved in the problem practices?
- if the objects were different would the essence of the problem be different?
- if the same object/technology was consumed or used differently, would the basic problem change?
- can those objects themselves be altered (by whom, at what cost, and long term or short term)?
- can the production, distribution, access and usage practices of those objects be shifted? If so, how?

The rule of thumb that arises from the above discussion is: whenever a social practice as entity is to be changed, there are (material and immaterial) objects involved. For the change to occur and persevere something must alter in the relationship (either acquisition, adoption, usage, sharing or disposal) between the key actors of the programme and the key objects. If only other elements of practice (skills, understandings, meanings and know-how) are addressed and objects are ignored, it is likely that changes in practices will be minimal or transitory.

Although it is obviously impossible to fully cover the endless and multifarious world of objects, it must be noted (perhaps muddying the waters even further) that individual product improvements, innovations or regulations that may seem to offer more or less temporary solutions to problems are only part of the story, and sometimes even quick fixes that only scratch the surface. To fully implement the social practice-based approach, system re-design, i.e., an entire transition of production-distribution-consumption systems, could be argued for. Ambitious visions of a *circular economy*, which re-uses both biological and technical 'nutrients' in safe ways and is modelled on the circle, not on a linear system, have been around for decades, but sustainable transition is slow and immensely complicated. Fossil fuel-based, 'cradle-to-grave' economic models are still the norm in spite of the significant (if trend-setting or not, it is too early to tell) Rockefeller Fund divestment from fossil fuels in autumn 2014 (Schwartz, 2014). For most readers of this book, system changing seems too formidable a task, yet sometimes dreaming about the ideal future can be an illuminating exercise. 'Back-casting' workshops are one method that can be used to work backwards from the ideal to reality, to plot a pathway or scenario of how to get to the desired future.

4.2.3 Regulatory environment

In Chapter 3, section 3.2, we introduced the socio-material network, which organises social practices. Practices are coordinated through normative prescriptions that determine toleration limits or appropriate ways of doing something. This can be done through artefacts, narratives, unwritten rules or legal regulations. For a change of normality to occur, the practices of producers of material infrastructure and things have to be examined: producers' resistance to changes has its own rationale and thus laws may have to be amended.

Regulation takes different forms, from 'direct' prohibitions on certain products and services to the legal framework that shapes the supply side of material infrastructure, products and technologies, in order to improve the availability of a product or to ensure informed decisions.

Modifying legislation is usually a long route that requires civic support, media advocacy, legal and area-specific expertise and political will. For example, the prototypes for self-extinguishing cigarettes were created in the USA at the end of the 1930s, but it took more than sixty years to legalise their manufacture in the US, EU and many other countries (National Fire Protection Association, n.d.). The time-line is shown in Figure 4.4. The main reason for the delay was the active lobbying by the cigarette industry. When civic activists resorted to fire accident data and legal arguments in their primary media message – deaths in fire accidents are often caused by burning cigarettes – producers launched consumer education initiatives stressing individual responsibility (Barbeau et al., 2005). The enforcement of the requirement was supported by civic activists, who worked with relevant officials, specialists and journalists state by state (McGuire, 1999). Also technical standards were put in place: a test that proved the likelihood of self-extinguishing. Passing laws often requires technical knowledge, negotiations and consultations, i.e., building a large coalition. For example, in Estonia, where careless smoking had caused 40–50 per cent of all fire deaths, the Estonian Rescue Board took the initiative (while the proposal still awaited EU-level technological

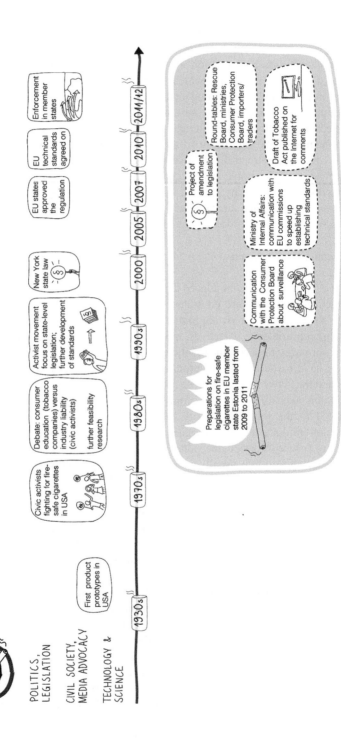

Figure 4.4   The creation of a regulatory framework for fire-safe cigarettes

standards) and started consultations with the Ministry of Social Affairs, responsible for tobacco policy, and organised a round-table discussion with representatives of ministries, the Consumer Protection Board and representatives of tobacco importers and retailers. The Ministry of Internal Affairs liaised with the relevant EU directorates in order to speed up the process of establishing technical standards. The draft amendment to the Tobacco Act was published on the Internet for public comment. As a result of all these activities, the key actors were prepared and, in autumn 2011, when the EU standards were finalised, Estonia was ready to adopt them immediately (see Figure 4.4). A year after the introduction of fire-safe cigarettes, the number of fire deaths had decreased by one-third (V. Murd, personal communication, 27 February 2013).

There are various ways of initiating or facilitating revisions to regulations. The following is a brief list of such possibilities.

The first involves using the existing possibilities of participating in policy making *at the level of executive power*. While procedures differ from country to country, in most democracies it is possible to:

- take part in preparing development plans, mainly through NGOs or as a representative of an interested party (e.g., parents' committees);
- take part in public discussions of plans and legal instruments;
- organise round-tables to discuss the matter with stakeholders;
- submit proposals and make enquiries;
- communicate with thematic and sector commissions and working groups in order to ask questions and submit proposals;
- raise the issue in the media (see below).

The method involves direct or indirect lobbying *at the level of legislatures*, for example to:

- inform or persuade a relevant politician or a party, communicate with advisers of factions and commissions, and seek an opportunity to speak in the parliament;
- organise discussions/round-tables/meetings and invite politicians, their advisers and representatives of the executive branch;
- introduce findings of surveys, and submit proposals to local and state authorities and parliamentary groups;
- co-operate with other organisers of campaigns and social change programmes, and respond to invitations to participate in those campaigns and programmes;
- contact local authorities or the parliament (to find a suitable commission or a friendly faction).

To raise the issue with *the media* and inform the *public*, it is possible to:

- organise signature collection campaigns;
- in the case of more emotional and large-scale problems of public interest, write (publicly) to the prime minister or the president;
- organise rallies;
- send public letters;
- analyse and criticise political platforms/policies;
- introduce survey findings by publishing press releases and organising seminars/workshops for the media;
- mobilise related groups to carry out joint actions (here social media provides many opportunities);
- analyse political opinions, make public the results of voting on specific questions and recognise politicians for their actions;
- organise protests.

Depending on the legal and monitoring systems of a country, it is worth investigating which authorities can be contacted (Chancellor of Justice, National Audit Office etc.). In the case of a serious legal issue, the dispute can be referred to a national or international court, such as the European Court of Justice in Luxembourg. Court decisions are interpreted and implemented in all EU member states the same way, i.e., national courts may not impose different sanctions for the same infringement. The European Court of Human Rights in Strasbourg has jurisdiction in all countries that have ratified the European Convention for the Protection of Human Rights and Fundamental Freedoms 1950 (ECHR).

The above-listed means are also useful in contributing to *policy making*. Policy is a principle of action of government, political party, business organisation etc. that states an aim and ways to achieve it (Anderson, 2005). Policy making begins with problem identification and agenda setting. Programme initiators can contribute significantly by raising issues in media and with the public. Agenda setting aims to demonstrate a possible solution to a problem, as well as to determine the key actors (often government) who have the relevant power. An agenda leads to the issue gaining momentum and priority over other topics due to public pressure from media or interest groups. The next step is policy formulation, where possible solutions and suitable instruments are established. The adoption of policy can lead to a new or changed law. Policy evaluation involves assessment of the effects of implemented measures. Programme initiators can give feedback on how tools have worked in a particular area.

While legal regulations can significantly transform the everyday environment, they are not sufficient to eradicate bad practices or to bring about changes in practices if the opportunity for debate and analysis is not offered.

4.3 Meanings

One of our basic premises is that holistic and integrative social change programmes need to address all practice elements to achieve durable practice change. Meanings are people's general understandings of what is entailed, for example, in being a good parent in a given society or in eating in a healthy manner, as well as more practical detailed know-how on how good parenting needs to be carried out in any particular family. Meanings mutate constantly and are, to some extent, responsive to change through deliberate planned communication.

4.3.1 Communication as a socio-material process

Social interaction is an integrative dynamic within practices linking them into meaningful arrangements and configurations. Although this falls in the section heading *Meanings*, more than understandings and ideas can be influenced and transformed through communication. With some simplification it can be said that communication is the 'glue' that keeps practices together, contributes to their development and dissolution.

Before we plunge into guidance on communication planning – although offering no recipes for press release writing – there are a few more general, theory-driven matters to be addressed first. This book has voiced its scepticism about improving the world only through public awareness campaigns. Some brief references to the communication theoretical and empirical roots of this belief may be instructive.

Many economics- and (social) psychology-based accounts of behaviour proceed from the concept of the rational individual, as we discussed in Chapter 2. The basic assumption is the existence of a cognitive repository or portfolio of relevant attitudes and knowledge among consumers (see Warde and Southerton, 2012a) available when necessary to retrieve information to make a choice. Alan Warde and Dale Southerton (2012a) emphasise the strength of the mainstream 'portfolio model' (Whitford, 2002), in which many (consumption) activities are believed to be discrete rational information-and-values-based acts. Warde and Southerton (2012b) give a clear overview of different strands of theory and research in cognitive neuro-science and cultural theory (highly illuminating further reading is available for those interested), which all have 'in common … that they postulate low levels of conscious cognitive processing in advance of action and thoroughly dispense with value-led, deliberative explanations of what people do. They do suggest that more systematic attention should be given to the phenomenon of habituation – to routines, habits and conventions' (p. 16). They also stress the interconnection of the human mind and body and the outside environment in providing resources upon which thinking draws by using the term 'distributed cognition'. This brings us back to behavioural economics and the 'nudges' we looked at critically in earlier chapters. This approach also posits automatic and non-reflective behaviour as the default mode of action and thus advocates the 'choice architecture' that steers irrational people in directions that are actually in their best interest. However, this approach tackles individual behaviours and does not actively apply social practices as activity patterns.

However, the image of a mental portfolio, which needs to be filled with 'adequate' information in order to achieve the 'right' behaviour is not very helpful in designing durable change. Value–action gaps remain. People know about and believe in greenness and healthy eating, yet do not act accordingly. Their behaviours in the 'heat of everyday action' are far from rational and information based. For example, according to a comparative study on financial literacy conducted by the OECD in 2012, there is no connection between a high level of financial knowledge and reasonable financial behaviour in Estonia, and in some other countries (Atkinson and Messy, 2012). In other words, the attitude is 'I know what is right and how I should manage my finances, but I don't do it that way'.

The second brief detour into theory takes us to organisational communication scholars, who address the Communicative Constitution of Organisations (Ashcraft et al., 2009) and the socio-materiality of communication (Orlikowski, 2010). Even though our main focus of attention is not organisations, it is useful to refer to the first stream of theories and paraphrase the term into the Communicative Constitution of Social Change Programmes in order to sensitise campaigners to communicative messages everywhere and before, during and after programme making. Disciplinary and professional borderlines segregate communication into separate domains (corporate communication, public relations etc.), which is not completely justified, because communication occurs everywhere, not only in campaign posters, websites or press releases.

Communicative Constitution, although a complex approach, offers two basic tenets in our present context: programmes – from planning to implementation to evaluation – consist of and are constituted not only by, but *in* communication processes. The organisation scholars François Cooren, Timothy Kuhn, Joep Cornelissen and Timothy Clark (2011) claim that 'If organizations are indeed *communicatively* constituted, it means that one should examine what happens *in* and *through* communication to constitute, (re-)produce, or alter organizational forms and practices, whether these are policies, strategies, operations, values, (formal or informal) relations, or structures' (p. 1511). So the discursive practices and sense-making that take place during various stages of programme making, even if they are viewed as purely the in-house work of a team, significantly influence the creative and output parts of a programme. For example, we have stressed the need to form partnerships and coalitions, to involve key actors in programme building. All this is a communicative process, even if it is not targeted at the end-audience. If stakeholders have a key role to play in the programme (e.g., a school canteen or an organic vegetable provider), they have to adjust their own everyday practices to meet the needs of the programme. This may mean re-organisation of work routines which in its turn entails communicative efforts. To make the programme coalition align and to find a strategic fit between the practices of key actors, interaction is needed. So we encourage adopting a broad view of communication, as well as acknowledging its fundamental role in both programme preparation and creative implementation.

The second point we want to stress is the connection of *ideation* or signification (i.e., meaning-making through the use of signs and symbols, mostly language and various textual means) and the *materiality* of physical (or virtual in the case of information systems and technologies) objects and environments. Meaning is conveyed not only by human agents but also by non-human ones (Cooren et al., 2011). This seems obvious, for example, in commercial marketing. In order to sell a product, the product must be functional, well-designed and affordable, before considering good marketing communications with catchy slogans and attractive advertising campaigns. Actual hands-on consumption experience is the most powerful meaning creator. For example, in the workplace, the meaning of work is not only shaped by the official corporate mission statement, but also by many connected discursive and material factors, as shown in Figure 4.3. The same applies to social change programmes. Media relations are often necessary to create consumer buzz, but if we wish to achieve changes in people's everyday reality, relying only on (mass or social) media words and images is narrow and sometimes short-sighted.

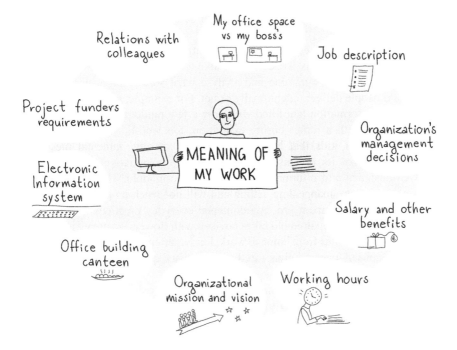

Figure 4.5   Formation of meaning

4.3.2 Providing information

If eco-labels and energy efficiency labels, for example, are introduced, obviously appropriate products are also needed. This requires thorough policy making to foster manufacturers' and sellers' initiative and co-operation in introducing more energy-efficient appliances. Information alone rarely changes long-term behaviours.

Many studies have revealed that well-targeted information increases consumer motivation to change behaviours (see e.g., Kastner and Matthies, 2014). It certainly may do so under some circumstances. But our book aims to examine behaviour change as an effort to modify, substitute or create new practices. Housing energy retrofit incentives are not about individuals or municipalities merely renovating houses, but about making living in such homes a standard, a normality. If an organisation only has the ability to spread information, allies and partners should be sought who can provide financial incentives, who can teach and train home-owners new skills, and who can provide affordable technologies and construction services. The home-owner is faced with a daunting array of details and nuances. Psychological individualistic accounts of behaviour change focus only on the behaviours that individuals engage in, but do not cover wider socio-material networks in which particular everyday practices are embedded. Our core message is that the campaign or programme should not be limited to disseminating words and pictures.

Nevertheless, effectively presented information is important. People attribute meaning to everything, as we discussed above. Thus it is worthwhile to map key elements of the programme and analyse what sort of messages activities, objects and people deliver, intentionally or not. For example, a rather nondescript conservation information tent filled with only a few random passers-by at a city handicraft fair with a rather boring exhibition, too well-lit for showing films, with activities for kids that have no connection to environmental messages, communicates that its organisers are not taking the initiative very seriously, and well-designed and informative leaflets may be ignored. The information is being offered in an unappealing setting and will not reach its audience, making it impossible to implement pro-environmental everyday practices. On the other hand, re-painted and repaired old bikes covered with flowers, scattered around the town on people's routes from home to work, kindergarten or shopping promoting a bike fair organised by eco-activists in the local artists' quarter may open powerful communication channels.

Various communication planning textbooks (see e.g., Wilson and Ogden, 2008) discuss tactics, i.e., how to choose the means to disseminate information. Therefore we will not go into detail here. We will present a few continua along which a variety of communicative methods can be assembled. The first is the personal/highly interactive communication (personal counselling, small-group seminars, e-mails etc.) versus mass produced and less interactive (such as social advertising on TV or posters in the street) continuum (see Figure 4.6). The size of the audience and the nature of the interaction is the basis for categorisation

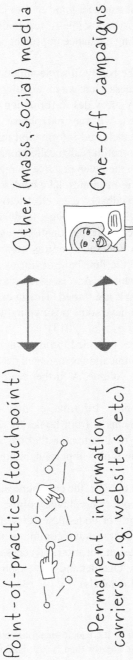

Personal, interactive (e-mails, seminars)

Point-of-practice (touchpoint)

Permanent information carriers (e.g. websites etc)

Online

Mass-produced, less interactive

Other (mass, social) media

One-off campaigns

Offline

Figure 4.6   Categorisation of communication tactics

here. As a general rule, impersonal media communication will not lead to any actual changes in practices, but it can be a good tool to create or increase public discussion. At the same time, it is impossible to reach all members of the target group personally. Therefore, finding a balance in project communication is one of the biggest challenges.

Another division that might be handy in some situations divides information provision by place and point of access. Here we may distinguish 'point-of-purchase communication', which actually provides information where the 'purchase' is made. For the present context, we may paraphrase it as 'point-of-practice communication': various signs, labels and information materials that are located at the crucial points of contact (sometimes also called touch-points) where people do things that are most relevant to the given practice change: buy vegetables, light their cigarettes, switch on washing machines, take bank loans or pour their wine. Various types of consumption feedback, e.g., electricity usage or eco-driving, can also be categorised here. Electricity usage feedback may be considered a very technologically advanced and personalised way of communicating, and often household usage data and social norms communication (how much others consume, the average and the threshold of, for example, environmentally damaging consumption) are combined. As discussed above, research results on the effectiveness of such feedback are varied. However, the existence of such information is generally found to have some positive influence on user behaviour (see e.g., Dogan et al., 2014; Harries et al., 2013).

Opposed to these are messages provided through various media (from TV to Facebook). How mediated communication is managed deserves separate attention as it is outside the scope of this volume. A further reading list is given for the interested reader.

The third division is temporal. Information may be amalgamated into permanent information environments – from books to websites – or they may be more short-lived, in the form of a campaign that has particular start and end points. The online–offline division is also important, although it seems that online communication is ubiquitous.

In choosing between different options, the communication planner's challenge is to keep materiality in mind from two vantage points: how the materiality of people's actual experience supports or undermines disseminated communication messages, and the fact that each act or event of communication has a materiality of its own; for example, the visual design, location and accessibility of labels, posters or websites are important (see e.g., Ölander and Thøgersen (2014) on the design of EU energy efficiency categorisation labels).

Think and stretch

Think of communication tactics (in all their socio-material versatility) that are needed to realise a programme meant for elderly men, who should visit the GP (general medical practitioner) once every two years as a regular prevention measure.

In the case of social change programmes, we can also distinguish between three general levels of providing information:

1. communicating with the key target groups or beneficiaries of a programme
2. being sensitive and meaningful in communication with key actors (especially direct coalition partners). The communicative constitution of the programme is relevant at every step.
3. informing the general public about the existence, initiators and objectives of a programme. Here a word of caution is in order. It can happen that the cart is put before the horse: communication about the launch and progress of the programme can overshadow its substantial messages to the actual beneficiaries of the programme. A government-initiated financial literacy strategy team may appoint the ministry PR team to handle the 'programme communications', which may end up being a stream of press releases, Facebook posts or tweets about another meeting of the steering committee. For some intra-coalition or political reasons, such an accumulation of symbolic capital may be relevant, yet the actual audience, let's say financially less capable young people, do not care about these meetings. So the reification of the programme into an entity that produces work and benefits for the programme team can even become a detriment to the real programme communication with its target audiences and it is necessary to ponder how this can be avoided.

Think and stretch

The government has adopted a national financial literacy strategy. In your opinion, which is more difficult: getting the press to write about the problem (as it is not very newsworthy, being multi-faceted and complex to analyse) or making journalists aware of the programme (which does not solve the problem)? Where should you invest the most effort?

In today's mediatised world (see Hjarvard, 2008; Krotz, 2007), where according to some theorists media actually mould the internal processes of various fields of life, from politics to culture, it is easy to consider the media and journalists as specific target groups of the social change programme. The social media era has made it possible for every initiative to set up a media channel of its own, whether on Youtube or Twitter, which is followed both by professional journalists and the general interested public. This can be viewed as a two-edged sword: on the one hand, communicative possibilities seem endless, and actual and potential public attention has been obtained by organisations or projects that otherwise would go unnoticed and where social media provide permanent virtual space for creating a stream of communication. On the other hand, the social media are full of noise and clutter and creating any interest there is exceedingly difficult. Also mediatisation, at its extremes, may create the impression of people's lives being lived from, by and in the media, which may bring about a false impression of the lessening importance of material, bodily realities in the 'offline' world. The Facebook community Healthier Estonia (https://www.facebook.com/hoolime), or Drink Half Less (https://www.facebook.com/joomepoolevahem), is a worthy initiative, yet its owners and designers face the constant challenge of navigating between virtual communication and the actual objective of the programme, which is making people consume less alcohol in their daily lives, which is indeed a socio-cultural, but also a very physical and material activity.

Communication must be planned *purposefully*, yet each programme designer has to live with the *complexity and ambivalence* of communication, i.e., one should always plan communication in advance, but must be aware of the limited capacity to control actual sense-making, let alone the ensuing behaviour.

This does not lessen the value of the golden rules of public relations: the main messages should be *clear and meaningful* to audiences (even if there is no intention to use the media). Every member of the project team should be ready to explain what they are doing and why. It may be unrealistic to make a whole, in some cases loose, coalition of programme partners speak with one voice, but at least the core team should have the rationale for beneficiaries formulated and memorised. This reduces complexity and increases the chances of making oneself heard in the clamour of thousands of messages begging for attention.

It can take a considerable effort to *translate* technical, scientific or bureaucratic language into words, images and material objects that are understandable and relevant to those the project is aimed at. Sometimes a facilitator, who can build bridges and feels at home in several domains, has to be employed. Often those who create new values and knowledge (for example scientists, engineers or artists) are poor communicators because 'translating' into layman's language may seem to dilute the value of an issue, as well as experts' symbolic capital. Professionals value the honour (and power) of their trades, and a specific language is often part of this. It is very hard for a natural scientist, doctor or lawyer to forgo jargon. Investing in 'translation' efforts is essential, or at least one should be prepared for the fact that on some occasions the same words mean different things to different people.

4.3.3. Advertising

Advertising is one of the most conspicuous means of communication used by social change programmes. Similarly to commercial advertising, public awareness advertising[2] is mediated, one-sided communication, which aims to convince the audience that something is beneficial or harmful, and often exaggeration or simplified connections, explanations and solutions are used.

---

2   There is no single term for advertising that focuses on social issues. It is called 'public service announcement', 'public sector advertising', 'charity advertising', or 'non-profit firms' advertising'. The term 'social advertising' was also used before commercial advertising in social media networks became widespread.

Figure 4.7 **Public awareness messages calling for re-use from the Second World War (left) and today (right)**
Reprinted under the Creative Commons licence, photo on the right by Kevin Dooley

The role of advertising in the gradual changing of social norms is noteworthy. Advertisements are deeply ingrained in our everyday life (Cook, 2001) and they form a natural part of our common cultural landscape, similarly to street signs, newspapers and Facebook postings. We actively use advertising in our everyday practices (O'Donohoe, 1994) to interpret phenomena, as something to talk about and as a means of producing the feeling of belonging.

Think and stretch

Look at the images in Figure 4.7. How have social norms and the wider socio-material network related to the idea of buying new things less frequently (by re-using them) changed?

One way to 'normalise' the (shift in) meanings represented in the advertisements is through their reproduction by the public. All advertisers strive to make their messages stick, to become objects of talk and reproduction. There are hundreds of parodies of ads posted on YouTube, some fashioned by advertisers themselves. Public sector organisations have invited users to create ads on the principle of co-production (Paek et al., 2011). However, it is not easy to make advertisements enter public conversations in today's densely-packed information environments.

Can an ad directly reform people's everyday practices? Some authors argue that the potential of advertising to do so is very limited (Ehrenberg, 1998; Jones, 1998). Some researchers believe that it has some capacity, for example reporting on how ads have changed children's eating habits (Hota et al., 2010) and on how they persuade older men to start being attentive to their wives' health and encourage them to see doctors (Buckley and Tuama, 2010). Definitely advertising is connected with the wider socio-material network that coordinates people's everyday practices. Ads that strongly contradict unwritten social norms are usually rejected. For example, the suggestion that girls should always have a condom close at hand in order to ensure safe sex may be resisted because cultural norms support male dominance in relationships: 'decent girls do not want to admit that they go out "hunting" for sex' (Hinsberg, 2011, p. 34).

To lead people to make an effort, ads often stress the unpleasant consequences of inaction. Fear as a bio-political technology used to promote healthy lifestyles has been criticised (Gagnon et al., 2010), because it generates ambiguity and insecurity in the target group. Public awareness campaigners have to consider that their messages shape the public 'pain threshold' and should avoid littering the public space with shocking content, because it de-sensitises viewers through emotional exhaustion. The very popular public awareness campaign 'Dumb Ways to Die' by Metro Trains (Australia) warns against ignoring signals at rail crossings (http://dumbwaystodie.com/). Its style is humorous and animated characters deliver warning messages. The video clip and song have been widely shared on social media and it has inspired dozens of parodies. Metro Trains claims that the campaign has led to real change: the share of 'near-miss' accidents with vehicles and pedestrians at rail crossings per million kilometres decreased from 13.29 to 9.17 during the year after the campaign was launched (Cauchi, 2013). As allowing a reprint of the image from the campaign in black and white was impossible for Metro, we advise the reader to take a break, switch to YouTube and watch the witty and amusing video together with its many reworkings by net users or download the mobile app and enjoy playing for a while.

Critics of advertising argue that advertisements treat the audience as mere consumers, casting them in passive and individualistic roles (Hove, 2009). While social advertising lays emphasis on the interests of society rather than on material benefits for the public, we side with the critics, at least partly. Social advertising offers benefits by making simplified, artistically exaggerated recommendations, but following the advice of an ad may prove stressful in everyday life. Therefore, advertising should be supported by other tools.

The use of social advertising is usually expensive and requires skill in briefing and negotiating. It is crucial that the programme initiator have a clear idea of the connections between the elements of practice change: meanings, skills, things and material infrastructure, and interaction between actors. Advertising can attract attention by constructing connotations that stand out from other messages in public space and link actors with the other tools of a change programme that are more context and situation specific. For example, if the idea is to train people to check how fire safe their homes are by using a check-list, then ads should focus on the check-list. It is essential to determine a coherent set of programme tools and subsequently define the objectives of advertising, not vice versa, i.e., adapting the programme tools to a cool advertising idea.

Public awareness advertising is an expanding domain; professional contests and festivals are organised to award creative solutions that sensitise public opinion to social issues.

A good brief that kick-starts co-operation with advertising professionals includes:

- *Background information.* This part gives the advertiser insight into the problem by referring to statistics, survey data etc., as well as examples from everyday life that illustrate the problematic practices (quotes from people involved, visuals etc.). Copy writers tend to live in a highly mediatised world and may be out of touch with target groups and problematic practices. It is extremely advisable to provide them with some ethnographic data. Depending on the subject, they should try to experience first-hand what the campaign wishes to advocate (having a healthy diet, no speeding on roads etc.) or make observations, watch good documentaries etc. That generates empathy, which catalyses ideas and avoids patronising, unnecessarily shocking or stereotyping story lines.
- *Objective of the specific advertisement.* What do we want the target group to do differently? This may be worked out in the course of discussions or brainstorming sessions between the creative team and the contracting

entity. It must have an outcome that can be clearly assessed. The effect is often too narrowly understood as a share of people who have seen the ad (measured in Target Rating Points or Gross Rating Points), but we suggest analysing also the 'connection points', where the ad links with the other tools of the programme (the number of queries, completed check-lists etc.). It is also important to explicate the long-term tasks or the whole context of the programme. For example, if your programme strives for collective, community level solutions, the advertising should try to persuade people not to be concerned only about their own health or safety, but also inquire whether their friends, (grand)parents and neighbours need assistance.

- *Target group(s)*. Defining the socio-demographic indicators (such as age and gender) is not enough. The copy writer has to put himself in the shoes of the target group (key actors), try to understand what its members care about or are afraid of, how they handle things etc. Interaction between the key actors and the multi-step communication effect is important as well. Also, not all of life takes place on the Internet: sharing 'a viral' with Facebook friends does not necessarily mean that people will actually change their practice.

- *Other aspects* related to the campaign or project include supporting information that the advertising agency should be aware of, for example listing other actions related to the project and relevant partners/stakeholders. Ideally, authors of advertisements organise communication events related to other processes and intentions of projects.

- *Timetable*. The timetable specifies which conceptual ideas, prototypes etc. should be completed by which deadline, and should contain an ample time reserve. The creators of advertising should not be allowed to dictate the pace of work. The advertising agency should also submit a *debrief* to ensure that the parties have understood each other correctly.

4.4 Skills and competences

Skills and know-how are cornerstones of social practices. Social change programmes that aim to create a new normality must ask a crucial question: can people do what is required of them and, if not, can they be educated and how? Meaningful activity – guided by both practical and discursive consciousness – is the greatest teacher. People learn by doing. An interesting practice-based conceptualisation of how learning takes place is outlined by Omar Lizardo (2009). The main starting point is that practices are, to a large extent, tacit; they build upon embodied know-how not easily transmitted by words or obtained by memorising, in the usual cognitive sense of the word. We discussed 'distributed cognition', involving brain, body and external environment, in Chapter 4, section 4.3.1. This resonates with Lizardo's 'practical socialisation'. Often teaching and learning (at least in the realm of formal education) are viewed as primarily linguistic and representational, i.e., based on transmitting explicit, mostly verbalised units of 'knowledge' that are cognitively internalised by students. Although this book cannot diverge into educational theory and contemporary didactic approaches, it is worth noting that activity-based, active learning is becoming more widespread and gaining momentum. Lizardo's reference to cognitive neuroscience, coupled with his account of practice theory, states that learning and socialisation take place, to a large extent, based on implicit, embodied representations, in which doing, a combination of physical and mental (but on the level of practical, not discursive consciousness) activity, is emphasised. Doing is often carried out with the help of imitation, based on the observation of the actions of other people. Riding a bike cannot be taught with the help of books or even training videos alone. People have to mount bikes and start pedalling, and acquire balance, as well as skills of coping in the flow of traffic.

Today's pedagogy places significant weight on *learning outcomes*, which are often expressed in terms of skills and competences that the student should acquire. In the present practice-based programme context, this means analysing necessary skills for practice change very closely. What must people be able to do, both mentally and physically, in order to eat more healthily or manage their personal finances in a more 'literate' way? In our experience, mental competences to think, analyse, read, verbalise etc. tend to form the bulk of various curricula and study plans. This may result in underrating material and bodily (sensory-motor) aspects of new or modified practices. To make a long story short, only telling people what they should know, think and do is not sufficient. Environments and spaces for trying new activities literally 'hands-on' by observing the doings of experts (e.g., cooking with organic vegetables or sharing household appliances in a community) are necessary for the practical socialisation of novices.

4.4.1 Education, curricula and study materials

Let's have a look at the basic contours of educational systems and means, i.e., how learning can be facilitated and accelerated. Many programmes cited in this book involve the notion of *consumer education*, in itself a hybrid of formal school-based education (see below), non-formal education and learning-by-doing. The official definition of consumer education by the European Commission is broad and can encompass basically anything: 'Consumer Education is concerned with teaching people the skills, attitudes and knowledge required for living in a consumer society. It is a fundamental component of general education, which should support consumers in their attempts to organise their everyday lives in a sustainable way' (Consumer Classroom, n.d.). It is not surprising that this definition is deeply rooted in the individualist paradigm, yet it is encouraging that skills are emphasised, not knowledge or attitudes. In this connection, two basic questions surface: how can we make practitioners adopt skills necessary for new practices, and how can we make these people transmit those skills and become the nodes from which the new normality can spawn?

From the point of view of the programme designer, various *categories of education* can come into play:

(1) *formal education*, or education provided by educational institutions based on curricula, (2) *non-formal education*, or clearly defined and purposeful extracurricular activities carried out at educational institutions, and (3) *informal education*, learning processes outside educational institutions, i.e., encountered in the course of everyday life and work. The interventions described in this textbook may take place in any of the three settings. Programme designers have to reflect on viable options of teaching on the continuum from formal (state) curricula to one-off seminars and training sessions, internships and other hands-on ways of learning (more on those in the next section).

Which level of education (primary, secondary or tertiary) is pertinent depends on the programme target audience. What is already included in the official curricula? What is integrated into the existing school programmes and lessons? Are there sufficiently trained teachers and what are their teaching habits? If the existing curricula do not cover the target issue (e.g., personal finance and overall financial literacy), what are the opportunities for inclusion?

One option is that the existing teaching staff incorporate the topic into their lessons. This is usually a long-term and gradual process. Attempts to include personal finance in the National Curriculum of England by the Personal Finance Education Group (http://www.pfeg.com) in the UK is an instructive example. Teachers are busy and curricula are often overloaded. It is not easy to introduce financial literacy topics into civics or mathematics courses overnight. Considerable preparatory work may need to be done. In many countries, national curricula offer ample leeway for schools to devise their own programmes, so it may be a useful idea to work with some pilot schools as a test ground and then move on based on that experience.

Co-operation between schools and various authorities, NGOs and other actors, where responsibilities of teaching are shared, can also be a good way forward, as relying on school teachers only can be a non-sustainable track, because of their too busy schedules.

For example, the concept Me & MyCity is a unique educational module developed and used in Finland (http://www.yrityskyla.fi). It is co-funded by the Finnish Ministry of Education and Culture, local authorities, various funds and enterprises. It is a comprehensive programme to teach sixth-formers entrepreneurship, responsible consumption and active citizenship. The Me & MyCity website describes the programme: 'The Me & MyCity learning environment is a miniature town where students spend a day as employees, citizens and consumers. The learning environment includes 15–20 companies from various sectors. The student assignments are based on the operations of real companies. The companies may vary regionally' (Yrityskylä, 2014). Pupils actually taking up the roles of professionals and consumers, spending their day in a realistic, material (not only digital) mini-town, resonates well with the practice-based framework.

Figure 4.8   The 'Me & MyCity' learning environment
Reprinted with the permission of Yrityskylä / Me & MyCity. Photo by Kalle Wilkman

However, formal education mostly reaches children and school age youth, who can be a deceptively easy to define target group. Small age differences and varying socio-economic backgrounds mean a lot, so there is no uniform 'children and youth' category. Schools are strong coordinating powers of many youth practices, both positive (e.g., learning and hobby activities) and negative (school violence). If the key actors and audiences are not children and youth, relying only on schools can be a waste of time, as the young may have no opportunities to implement their newly acquired skills, or can produce results only over many years, so they cannot be assessed by the programme evaluator. Sociologists call the phenomenon where the young teach the old 'reverse socialisation' (mainly referring to the digital generations being smarter than their parents in IT-related issues; see Livingstone and Bober, 2005), and the results of this may also take too long to emerge.

Since education is a huge field governed by strong traditions and norms, it is rather easy to be carried away by the power of the field and start treating teaching and classrooms as magic wands that can generate future desirable practices. But if we turn the problem around and start back-casting from the desired practice as an assemblage of different elements, skills among them, it is helpful, though sometimes uncomfortable, to ask who needs to know and master exactly what sort of competences. Are those competences fully predictable and unequivocal or is there a fair amount of ambivalence involved? Practice-based programme design tends to – at least in the planning and perhaps 'dreaming' phase – think bigger than just one project. Thus the key question is not about school curricula or lesson plans (at least not at the beginning). What skills are needed by the practice to flourish can be a more provocative way of putting it, only then 'translating' these practice building blocks into learning outcomes.

Study Materials The amount of written and audiovisual materials meant to aid both teachers and learners is massive. Such materials are seemingly easy to devise, and many NGOs and public authorities produce them as part of their consumer education efforts. One of the most impressive EU-level collections is the website consumerclassroom.eu, where teaching kits and resources are available in all EU languages. However, teachers in many countries frequently complain that they do not have enough material to cover topics that fall more or less 'outside' the main national curriculum prescriptions. So, paradoxically materials and teachers often do not meet.

Thus the programme designers – if they opt for a package of materials for the classroom – should first and foremost consult the teachers about the form and substance of materials. Although such a liaison with actual pedagogical staff and dealing with national curricula are inevitable, there are potential pitfalls. With practice-based programme making, the desired practices should be the foci. This might get lost in the sometimes rigid and conservative teaching and school conventions, i.e., materials proceed from the requirements of classroom and curriculum, not necessarily embracing the actual skills needed for practice change. The primary learning outcome is the new/modified practice, which leads to the following key question: *which skills (both physical and mental) are needed for the desired practice* (e.g., safer behaviour on the roads or healthier eating) and how can teachers and study materials promote and support them?

Today's information-overloaded environment, busy lifestyles and constant multitasking mean that, in addition to books and longer written texts, brief handy versions that can be embedded into practice as real-life action guides (e.g., mobile apps and pocket guides) can be useful. This also entails making the materials easily searchable and available on the Internet with the help of Search Engine Optimisation. All this should not be misinterpreted as a call to abandon books, but rather should be seen as an attempt to encourage thinking about information consumption habits within real-life practices, on the go and on the ground level.

Last but not least, for any educational institution solving a social problem, schooling and disseminating knowledge form only one side of the coin. Even more important is how schools actually live and incarnate lifestyles and values they wish to advance. Learning experience is a multi-faceted and not only cognitive process, as was discussed above. Schools' everyday life – how basic practices of democracy and student engagement, tolerance, sustainable consumption and development are lived there in mundane micro-level doings – is an influential teacher in itself.

> **Think and stretch**
> *Financial literacy ABC* is a book meant for secondary schools, and is co-authored and sponsored by the National Bank and Ministry of Finance. It is freely available on the web as a pdf. How can you make school teachers actually use it in the classroom (bear in mind that financial literacy is not a separate learning outcome in the national secondary school curriculum)?

4.4.2 Training and personal consulting

One of the biggest effects of any formal education system is the socialisation of individuals to thinking and interaction performances. This is mostly appropriate with young people. However, present day *life politics* also sets growing demands on the development of skills of grown-ups. To fill this need, various programmes of non-formal education are offered.

The first challenge for training programmes is their short duration. As practices are routinised behaviours (Reckwitz, 2002), routines can hardly become established during an ordinary brief training schedule. But the advantage of the short amount of time is the possibility of playing with the methods of informal education and, if needed, making the methodology of teaching more flexible than in the formal education system.

The second challenge is to divide the practice of teaching from the practice of learning. Although it is still common to assume that a learner will save new information in his head in order to deliver it to others or to implement it in practice, this is insufficient in the practice-oriented approach to training programmes. Although there is a specific practice of 'participating in trainings' (for example, disruption of ordinary work flow, changing the context of conduct, specific scheduling, coffee breaks, and rituals of entering and closing), there is no one specific practice of learning. The nature of learning is situated, and secondary rather than primary. For example, by taking part in a training programme that is badly organised, the participant will learn little about the subject of the training, but a lot about the organisation of the training.

According to the well-known book about situated learning by Jean Lave and Etienne Wenger (1991/2003), the teacher may have an idea about an advisable practice, but he is not able to pass on his representation of it to the learner directly. And, *vice versa*, the learner understands the nature of the teacher's performances only in his own way; he picks up bits of knowledge that can be reconciled with his earlier understandings. Therefore, although the performances of the teacher and learner in a workshop may seem similar, their understandings of the practice remain far apart.

According to Lave and Wenger (1991/2003), learning takes place within the social engagements that provide variability of understanding within situations. Learning is thus not a direct adoption of social procedures, but co-participation in the determination of their variability, i.e., learning comes from seeing somebody doing something differently. The direction of performance transfer (from the trainer to the trainee or *vice versa*) and its outcomes also depend on the learning situation and the range of contexts these are meant to describe. For example, learning will more likely take place by the patient rather than the doctor, and contact between equals in the same field of practice may be more egalitarian, but less fruitful due to the similarities of their practice.

Although the main thrust of Lave and Wenger's work (1991/2003) is to explain how newcomers become old-timers in a community of practice within co-participatory situations, they also emphasise that there are many newcomers who do not plan to achieve mastery of practice in the field. Instead, they pick up a few new skills and move on to other spheres of life to share their performance ability in new situational contexts. This is the way that the idea of training moved out of the field of sports into the field of management. Therefore, those who abandon the road to the mastery of practice are not necessarily less skilful learners. As William Hanks (2003, p. 24) put it in his foreword: 'Learning is a way of being in the world, not coming to know about it'.

In a practice change programme, training should be tied to the needs of key actors. Some possibilities are offered in Table 4.2.

Think and stretch
Devise a training programme for salespeople of consumer goods in regular shops; they should interact in sales situations with their customers regarding customers' two-year right of complaint.

To enhance learning, the following principles could come in handy:

- not filling up the whole course with extensive knowledge transfer that involves recording many different units, instead focusing on some units or enabling variability of attention among these for different trainees;
- instead of a very broad scope of information, repetition of single and contextual pieces of know-how within different situations;
- as the representation of performance is situational, helping the trainees to seek information on their own, or recommending study resources;
- focusing on hands-on participation, testing the desired activities in diverse contexts (e.g., what it means to be old or handicapped);
- gathering representatives of different fields of practice, and forming groups that help them to notice the variance between each other's routines;
- emphasis on embodiment, providing the trainees with versatile sensual experience: bodily movements, taste and smell, texture and colour, and related social interaction;
- rearranging or switching the training room. Reduce trainings within ordinary classrooms where the bodily and mental experience has no contact with what the training is about;

Table 4.2   Possible outcomes for a training programme

Outcome of the training	Who to address?
Imitation: Although most of the strategic plans demand the rise of analytic skills in society, the ability to imitate is a suitable outcome of the training, as the ability to learn develops in line with the ability to perform tasks. Imitation helps the participants to find natural ways of accommodation of the learned performance in their tense network of practices. The socio-material environment of the trainee should respond to the needs of the trainee. For example, the availability of products for organic cooking is sufficient.	*Practitioners with a similar challenge*, e.g., members of an organisation who have to be involved in waste recycling. Socialisation of *newcomers* to an organisation or a community of practice. *Key actors who trigger the change* in practice networks and influence others (who *nudges* performances), e.g., the director, the cook, the cleaning lady *Practitioners with a similar mission*, or experience in the same field, e.g., environmental civic initiatives.
Analysis and improvement: analysis of existing performances to find out what impedes the achievement of advisable results is not possible in the imitation phase. The old-timers of different communities of practice can safely question existing prescriptions and offer new ones. Mentoring (from the master to the apprentice), supervision (correspondence to professional standards, input to service improvement, etc.), coaching (an external expert encourages his trainees to find personalised ways out of their problems), etc. may be employed. These approaches focus on testing and accommodating of new performances in real life.	*Coalition partners*, who can offer congruent solutions, e.g., in the case of organic farming those who can provide individuals with training in cooking, products, recipes, points of purchase. *Organisations with the same target group*, interlocking organisations, e.g., re-use workshops, second-hand shops, old furniture reclamation groups
Co-creation: this outcome is good to cross over the boundaries of professional practice – to build links between different, but interdependent fields of practice, to think out of the box, to test and play with socio-material environment.	

- creating 'nudges' that will interrupt the natural ways of rehearsing a practice, analysing how the desired activity can be adapted in constrained circumstances (e.g., how to bake without wheat flour);
- providing non-mediated experience of the problematic practice (e.g., change the roles of the client and the service-provider).

Personal advice most often addresses particular skills that people need to master in order to make changes in their lives. For a social change programme, this is a very individual-centred and therefore expensive approach. However, it has great potential to be effective. Being confronted with new information and a feeling of uncertainty, actors are not satisfied with universal instructions (even if they are very clear) but search for sources that offer situationally (more) customised information (Lubi et al., 2014; Vihalemm et al., 2012). Broad coalitions with state or municipal authorities, as well as specific charities that provide certain services, can make this strategy more viable in the long term. Local social workers, for example, can be trained to provide financial capability advice to their clients, or family doctors can consult on nutrition. The wide spread of ICT solutions makes it possible to use web-based personal counselling in the form of real-time interaction or over a short time span (e.g., through an exchange of e-mails) on various topics, e.g., fire safety advice and discussion of health-related problems. Although health professionals question the quality of e-counselling, the beneficiaries themselves value it for its anonymity and easy access (e.g., Glarace et al., 2011). Setting up such counselling networks means that their long-term sustainability should be ensured, providing adequate financing and preparation of professionals. One-to-one conversations and tailored consulting can be very powerful in changing individual lives. Yet, if a conscious practice change endeavour is implemented, personal consultation needs to be supported by a mix of other measures.

4.5 New initiatives: social innovation

A new notion that is gaining popularity throughout the world is *social innovation*. This rather fuzzy concept can be defined in various ways, but one of the most well-known definitions states: 'We define social innovation as the development and implementation of new ideas (products, services and models) to meet social needs. In other words, they are innovations that are both good for society and enhance society's capacity to act' (Murray et al., 2010, p. 3). These are new initiatives whose common denominators are addressing a social problem or need and the renewal of social relations. True social innovation is not a change in fashion, but the emergence of new social practices (Gronow, 2009). One of the European Commission's Social Innovation Competition winners is the Urban Farm Lease in Belgium, which organises gardening and cultivation of horticultural crops in the urban environment and recruits unemployed people (European Social Innovation Competition, 2014a). The elements of the programme are still evolving, but the contours of the novel practices have already been outlined, along with potential difficulties, such as the lack of skilled people in urban gardening who could train workers.

The European policy document 'Empowering People, Driving Change. Social Innovation in the European Union' (Bureau of European Policy Advisers, 2011) classifies social innovations into three broad categories:

- Social innovations that respond to pressing *social demands* and are generally instigated by grass-roots organisations or groups. Private and public sectors both have roles in these initiatives. These innovations are aimed at filling gaps that have emerged due to limited resources of markets and states to address problems, and are geared towards vulnerable groups in society (such as the elderly, school drop-outs or disabled people);
- The second, broader level addresses *societal challenges* in which the boundary between 'social' and 'economic' blurs. Here, the central actors are often enterprises. This involves not only social responsibility campaigns by private firms, but a broader shift towards redefining values, adding the social dimension (e.g., human relations and social cohesion, or nature conservation) to economic benefits. This approach not only pursues business ends, but tries to fundamentally redefine the creation of benefits in modern society. Governments (e.g., in the US and UK) have made attempts to catalyse social entrepreneurs, charity organisations etc. into the re-design and running of public services, with the aim of not only finding ways to spend public money more effectively (the main pillar of the *outsourcing* strategy), but also transforming public services themselves (*The Economist*, 2010). This is well-known in the US, where social innovation is mostly understood as *social entrepreneurship* (e.g., Social Innovation News (http://www.socialinnovationnews.com); Stanford Social Innovation Review (http://www.ssireview.org/)).
- The third and most ambitious approach builds on the previous ones and aspires to achieve *sustainable and systematic social change* in order to improve the way people live and work in the broadest sense, by creating new mechanisms of empowerment, new social networks and learning opportunities. Naturally, this category primarily includes large-scale innovations that cover all sectors of society and are launched by policy-makers who embrace a number of different stakeholders. In the EU this category is the main focus of social innovation receiving research and development funding (e.g., Bureau of European Policy Advisers, 2011; Social Innovator (http://www.socialinnovator.info/)).

In the broadest sense, social innovation is an inspirational way of thinking and many social change programmes, projects and initiatives can be classified, directly or indirectly, as social innovations. The term is also used to indicate *methods and procedures* of generating ideas, such as various techniques of *co-creation*. These methods can also be employed in planning a traditional campaign and they may generate unexpected creative ideas. It is always instructive to ask what can be done, besides informing and calling for action, to encourage a target group to (self)-organise into social and co-operation networks. Innovative ideas may not pop up at a brainstorming session, but they can emerge when people going about their daily business meet unexpected obstacles or new people from other backgrounds are invited in. It is very important to notice these little moments of inspiration and listen to 'odd' questions posed by people who do not know 'how things have always worked'. The co-creation and involvement of programme beneficiaries is often talked about, but difficult to realise, because it is hard to get people together, group dynamics may work counter-productively, and it takes immense moderating skill to steer a fuzzy conversation to an efficient end. Thus there is a temptation to replace true co-creating and crowd-sourcing with 'marketing' of the solutions developed by experts for users, which brings about 'pseudo-involvement'.

Social innovations also occur inside organisations that initiate them. Thus it is important to be ready for one's own organisation's practice change. If it is not feasible to bring all ideally relevant parties to one table, efforts should be made to invite the maximum number of parties with whom it is conceivable to co-operate. The material environment of the endeavour is very important. Social innovation is not just beautiful thoughts and words, but also requires tackling material issues that may not be innovative at all.

The process of social innovation can be divided into the following six stages (adapted from Murray et al., 2010):

1. *Prompts, inspirations and diagnoses*. At this stage, we look at the indicators that highlight the need for innovation from an imaginative angle, such as new research findings, public spending cuts and crises. We recommend using a practice-based approach to diagnose the problem. As discussed in Chapter 3, it is crucial to have a good understanding of the everyday life of the target group by trying to experience it first-hand and/or by using research (ethnographic) methods in order to diagnose problems and their causes. The trigger of a search for a solution to accumulated problems may be newly published research results, lack of funding, public debate etc. At this stage, two things are essential: 1) asking questions that help view things from another angle and 2) unleashing the creative potential of communities. The phrasing of the problem matters too. Overly technical or 'clinical' wordings, such as 'The problem is children's excessive consumption of sugar', or deficit-based sentences, such as 'The problem is people's lack of financial awareness' or 'The problem is funding cessation', may be used in some institutional circles, but these are not compatible with the practice change view of devising an actual programme. Formulations in everyday language, such as 'how easy and convenient is it to eat sweets or soft drinks instead of carrots?', 'does it really make sense to buy pension insurance if you currently cannot make ends meet?', or 'what will change in the world if this project no longer exists?' will push programme makers into everyday practice mode, bringing them more in touch with lay reality. Here are some simple techniques that will help on this journey:

- *visualisation:* highlighting the problem with free-hand drawings and images related to the problem;

- *first-hand trial:* finding out how and at what price the relevant goods and services are supplied and environments and events are organised; trying out solutions to the same problem offered by the public or private services;
- *potential coalition and competition analysis:* obtaining a few other project applications and blueprints and considering what benefits they provide and what the possibilities of synergy are;
- *observation and participation:* talking to and watching those who play a key role in problem formulation. Such project-based solutions as competitions and special gatherings provide an opportunity for communities that are already in contact and have reciprocal trust, but innovative potential can remain hidden when actors with no prior connection meet. Providing a common physical space to meet and arranging events where new actors in the field can meet may be helpful. It is believed that teams composed of people of very different (disciplinary) backgrounds are strong facilitators for solutions. However, studies (e.g., Majchrzak et al., 2012) show that specific proficiencies and techniques to make diverse teams work fruitfully are also required. Often a lot of energy is devoted to explaining specific phenomena or clarifying jargon within separate sectors. It is better to keep such introductions as brief and egalitarian as possible, leading to 'rising above differences', which entails finding workable metaphors and 'scaffoldings' that lift the team up instead of plunging them into the very time- and emotion-consuming process of resolving disciplinary or human differences. This helps to ensure some pragmatic common ground and highlights how each one can contribute in their respective roles, employing their valuable background know-how for the joint objective.

2. *Proposals and ideas.* This is the stage of idea generation. We recommend thinking outside the comfort zone (by using various methods that encourage ingenuity) and combining different techniques. As mentioned above, novel ideas might not emerge at formal brainstorming meetings. Instead they may pop up within other activities and unexpected situations and thus, unfortunately, be quickly forgotten. Therefore, we recommend starting idea pooling with warmups, where participants recall their experiences, switch roles and are playful. Also, it is vital to create 'storage space' for new ideas that surface while running a project: one might not have enough time to deal with them at the moment, but they might be valuable in future. It is doubtful whether a project-based approach is a suitable framework for truly new ideas, because projects foresee particular results. Instead, it might be smarter to consciously create a favourable environment for the emergence of new thinking without prescribing specific outcomes, for example by strengthening creative campuses or reforming project funding and accounting principles (Tago, 2014).

3. *Prototyping and pilots.* This is the phase where ideas are tested in practice. It provides feedback for the following stages and helps to set the stage for measuring

success. A critical review of the solutions offered and of their power to change practices is needed here. If a solution is designed for just one practice component, whether it is meanings, skills, things or interactions, it usually leads to 'business as usual' because social practices are often deeply ingrained and have strong inertia. Another weak point might be that the model is tested on an audience who are highly motivated or do not belong to the 'real' target group. Hence it is worthwhile: (a) to ensure that the model covers all the practice elements at least to some degree, (b) to focus on the 'difficult' target population, and (c) after the test period, to think critically about what should be revamped to guarantee the sustainability and resilience of the innovation among less motivated or lower-resource people.

4. *Sustaining*. This is when the idea takes root in everyday practice, becoming a normality. It is vital to find out what conditions the innovation requires to sustain itself and to communicate them to interested parties. Initiators have to find resources to safeguard the financial longevity of the initiative (this means identifying budgets, teams and complementary resources). Current programmes are largely project-based, i.e., resources are provided by donors (such as the EU) for a specified time and for certain work packages. This creates a challenge because social change, sustainable social relations and community co-operation cannot be produced in the course of one short-term project. It is in the interest of donors to fund sustainable projects, i.e., they are more willing to give money if they know what will happen after the project is completed. If the result of an initiative is a lasting practice or venue for people to meet, it is easier to find initial financing for the project.

5. *Scaling and diffusion*. While dissemination of an idea is not always the main objective, many good social innovations create greater social well-being if more people than the initial target participants benefit from them. An example of success is the cleaning action 'Let's do it!', an endeavour that has spread from Estonia to 96 countries (http://www.teemeara.ee). The authors of a new enterprise must create demand, either among end consumers or policy and decision makers, in order to up-scale and transfer to new contexts. While supportive communication plays a critical role here, it should not be understood only as public relations activities or (social) advertising campaigns in their narrow sense. More intimate dialogue that takes place face-to-face or through a social network (online or offline) is very important in circulating the idea and sharing experiences.

6. *Systemic change*. This is the ultimate goal of social innovation. However, the question that always arises is: which concrete (socio-technical) system do we want to change? This question needs to be addressed to define long-term objectives. However, each initiative has its own focus and it is impossible to change the whole social system with one brush stroke.

Think and stretch

One of the finalists of the European Social Innovation Competition was the web-based employment service AutieCorp, which mediates links between autistic people who have special talents; potential employers support these people with advice and information (e.g., how employees can make easy adjustments to work environments) (European Social Innovation Competition, 2014b). The AutieCorp is run by autistic people. AutieCorp's goal is to show that autism can be an advantage, not a disability. The current service is in the *prototyping and pilots* stage, with a few actions under way and the ambition of spreading internationally. What would help the service to move forward into the *sustaining and diffusion* stages?

4.6 Programme implementation

Although detailed tactical assistance is beyond the scope of this book, the question of how to actually implement a programme is important. Therefore, this section provides a few general, down-to-earth suggestions and survival tips instead of operational knowledge on media relations, lobbying or co-operation with product innovators, which all deserve separate volumes. We assume that the reader knows best about the actual methods of programme design in their domains; our aim is to offer some useful ideas in the framework of social practice-based thinking.

Each small section poses a fundamental question, followed by a few brief bullet points that provide some guidance.

How can we assess programme implementation risks and potential sustainability?

- Before the actual programme launch, time should be taken to evaluate the feasibility of all the activities planned in terms of money, time and competence. Ideally, this *risk-analysis exercise* is done with coalition partners.
- There is a fine *balance* between fulfilling the project requirements (which may easily drown in bureaucracy) and the initiators' creative ideas. Maintaining at least a spark of ingenuity and free thought within an institutional maze is vital because a practice-based programme requires vision and courage.
- The coalition team's human interaction is the key to success. There is always a threat of burn-out. Therefore it is crucial to create *oases of free exchange of ideas* and some relaxation within the programme, as these safety valves make it possible to assess the programme without being too judgemental and to spark new ideas.
- The whole ideology of a practice-based social change programme is centred on *durability and resilience*, i.e., the new practices should take root like the perennial plants we talked about earlier. Thus some serious thought needs to be given to what the programme's key actors will do after

the project, or a specific stage, is finished. How can the new or modified practices reproduce themselves without constant 'energy-injection' from yet another programme?

How can we compile a sustainable and feasible programme?

- In real life, programme design mostly boils down to *resources*. Even if the programme is strongly limited by the funders' requirements, it is worthwhile looking at the objectives and goals foreseen by funders with a critical eye. How much *space of interpretation* is there?
- Often programmes consist of *outsourced activities*. Generally, outsourcing is most effective with work packages that have relatively simple goals, and are concrete and measurable. Very complicated ongoing processes (e.g., communication with coalition partners or the media) should not be delegated to outside parties.
- *Integration of programme elements* is vital. Although this has been covered by numerous 'integrated marketing communications' books, we use it here in a rather different light. The foundations for programme cohesion are the desired practices: their meanings, skills and materials, as well as interactions we wish to induce between relevant key actors. Thus all kinds of exercises, including visualisations that map the whole territory 'inhabited' by the desired practices and their elements, serve as the core guide for selecting proper methods. All practice elements should be either directly covered (e.g., skills – training sessions, and meaning – media communication) or at least indirectly supported.

As the next chapter will discuss, programme implementation, monitoring and even some ongoing evaluation go hand in hand, so it is advisable to create some distance (do something else for a change) and then address the following questions:

1. So far how much does the programme allow for the possible *counter-pressure* of various socio-cultural and economic environments, i.e., how much do the key actors' everyday routines impede the programme? Where are the spaces of opportunity to galvanise the most synergy and potentially best results?
2. Is the expected change well integrated with other supporting practices so that they can form a meaningful fabric in people's lives? Practices never live in isolation!

Innovative and complex programmes often tend to lose some of their punch because real life, with its – mainly resource-related – limits, demands adjustments. How can we ensure that the *original objectives of practice change* do not get distorted within the nitty-gritty of everyday project-management, yet *flexibility* and *adaptability to the shifts and fluctuations in the territory* are retained?

- It may well be that timetables and funders' requirements attach so many strings that the project leader's room to manoeuvre is minute. So each time a shift in programme activities or trajectory is called for, *risks need to be assessed*: is this change institutionally feasible, and what is the ratio of the programme change complexity to the real need to adjust and re-skill?
- Since most social change programmes tackle *wicked problems in open-ended territories*, generally each solution to the original problem engenders new problems and unintended side-effects. Sometimes it is necessary to fight and justify the need to adapt and change course; thus a long-term programme ideally is comprised of *stages*, between which there is time for analysis and gear-shifting if needed.
- One of the basic recommendations here is that real *ground-level fieldwork* has to be done not just after programme completion but also during it. The key people conducting the programme should, if at all possible socially, culturally and personally, put themselves in the shoes of programme beneficiaries, or at least take an ethnographic approach and try to gather as much first-hand experience and as many fresh impressions from people into whose lives the programme intervenes as possible.

4.7 Summary

In this chapter, the practice elements model is put to work in programme design and implementation. All social practices co-evolve within material and physical infrastructures, environments and sets of products and artefacts. How much investment can be put into environment re-design or innovation depends on available resources. The cost of changing the material reality can be daunting compared to an awareness campaign, so smart coalitions and partnerships between the public sector, businesses and NGOs are best. The scale of change varies from small incremental additions to existing products and environments to complete infrastructure re-design (which is bound to be a high-level integrated policy effort). When contemplating the development of material artefacts, a continuum ranging from risky items as focal points of the problematic practice to items as supportive of the problematic/desired practice is provided. In the former case, stronger regulatory and economic means (e.g., bans on alcohol) may be morally more justified in many contemporary societies, whereas products that cannot easily be labelled as problematic in themselves require a more complex set of measures. The third category that deserves attention here is utilities, notably energy, which is conceptualised as an 'ingredient' of social practices not as an end in itself.

Methods of modifying a regulatory environment include participating in policy making at the executive level, lobbying on the legislative level and using public attention and media to exert pressure on regulators.

Meanings are shaped in the socio-material totality of everyday life, not just in symbols and discourse; no linearity between providing information, persuading and calling to action can be presumed. The chapter proposes a wider view on communication: how meaning is constructed in cognition, body and environment interactions, and how a social change programme is constituted in communication processes of planning, negotiating with coalitions, making sense of implementation etc. This does not exclude careful contemplation and coordination of programme communication in the narrower sense of messages, channels and audiences. It often requires considerable effort to 'translate' between different discourses of experts and various lay audiences.

Advertising is a widely used behaviour change measure, whose efficacy should be analysed carefully. We see it more as a supportive method, rather than an engine of practice change on its own.

Skills and competences as practice components can be moulded through various means and techniques used in education and training. Active embodied learning combined with adoption of skills relevant for the desired practice is the key. Navigation and negotiation between the 'needs' of the desired practice and the rules and conventions of the sometimes conservative field of education can be challenging. Yet the strategic fit between the programme's goals and what can be taught in school or training sessions is essential, because teachers and trainers are crucial intermediaries on whom the success of the programme may depend if it has a strong educational element. The three primary outcomes of training are imitation, analysis and improvement, and co-creation.

In a way, the most ambitious programme design element is social innovation, which aims to further social good and create novel social relations and co-operation patterns. Different phases of social innovation include: prompts and diagnoses, idea generation, testing and prototyping, scaling and diffusing, and systemic change.

Implementation of the programme largely depends on the interaction of the project team and coalition partners, so spaces of free idea generation as safety valves, as well as breaks when intermediary programme performance monitoring can be conducted, are essential. Programme evaluation will be further examined in Chapter 5.

Further Reading

Beard, C. and Wilson, J. (2013). *Experiential learning: A best practice handbook for trainers and educators* (3rd ed.). London, England: Kogan Page.
Design Thinking for Educators (n.d.). Webpage introducing the design thinking for educators. Retrieved from http://www.designthinkingforeducators.com/
Lave, J. and Wenger, E. (eds) (1991/2003*). Situated learning. Legitimate peripheral participation.* Cambridge, England: Cambridge University Press.
Meroni, A. (ed.) (2007). Creative Communities. People inventing sustainable ways of living. Retrieved from https://archive.org/details/creative_communities

Murray, R., Caulier-Grice, J. and Mulgan, G. (2010). *The open book of social innovation*. Retrieved from http://www.nesta.org.uk/sites/default/files/the_open_book_of_social_innovation.pdf

Organization as Communication (n.d.). Webpage introducing the communicative constitution of organization. Retrieved from http://orgcom.wordpress.com

Putnam, L. and Mumby, D. (eds) (2014). *The Sage handbook of organizational communication*. London, England: Sage.

Ruckenstein, M., Suikkanen, J. and Tamminen, S. (2011). *Forget innovation. Focus on value creation*. Helsinki, Finland: Edita Publishing.

Social Innovation Europe (n.d.). Webpage introducing European social innovation ideas and activities. Retrieved from http://www.socialinnovationeurope.eu/

Social Innovator (n.d.). Webpage introducing mainly US social innovation ideas and activities. Retrieved from http://www.socialinnovator.info/

Southerton, D., McMeekin, A. and Evans, D. (2010). International review of behaviour change initiatives. Retrieved from http://www.scotland.gov.uk/Publications/2011/02/01104638/10

Strategic design scenarios (n.d.). Webpage introducing strategic design ideas, possibilities and tools. Retrieved from http://www.strategicdesignscenarios.net/category/library-menu/

Chapter 5

Programme evaluation

The aim of this chapter is to give some guidance on how to evaluate and measure programmes and how they are linked with the more general occurrence of social change. This chapter focuses on practice change, combining this approach with established traditions of impact evaluation. We distinguish between programme outputs, outcomes and impacts, while cautioning against attributing pure overall impact to particular interventions and establishing linear causal chains. The chapter touches upon such concepts as the provisional stability of the programme, and discusses issues related to viability. A multi-method and realistic approach is proposed that includes the main elements of social practices and their supporting socio-material networks in its evaluation efforts.

5.1 Making sense of programme evaluation

Non-profit organisations, social entrepreneurs and governmental authorities whose mission is social well-being and who directly, or sometimes inadvertently, engage in life politics have to document their work for financing bodies and partner organisations, as well as producing evidence on the effectiveness of their programmes. Producing evidence involves three questions: (1) what investments or *inputs* have been made in terms of time, money, materials, technologies etc. by programme initiators and coalition partners?; (2) what activities were carried out, what materials and environments were created, and what relations were established: what were the tangible and intangible *outputs* of the joint action?; and (3) how did the target group members respond and how did their lives change as an *outcome* of these actions? The difference between an *output* and an *outcome* is somewhat tricky. For example, a training course activity can be measured (a) as an *output*, by asking whether a training course was arranged and how many beneficiaries participated in it, and (b) as an *outcome*, by inquiring if beneficiaries acquired any new skills or improved existing ones. On the basis of the ratio of inputs and outputs, it is possible to calculate how reasonable the particular programme has been in its attempt to solve or alleviate a particular problem, both in terms of the relative benefit it brings in terms of the money spent, and in comparison with other similar efforts. If the programme is subjected to formal assessment by funders, professional external help should be considered (and necessary expenses should be planned in the budget), because evaluation of social impact/social value has become a practice with its own rules, procedures[1] and such items as special summary booklets.[2] In many countries, there are enterprises or civic organisations, who counsel about how to 'monetise' the results of programmes and/or offer relevant services. But programme initiators themselves have to decide what kind of evidence has to be collected and used as the basis of calculations. How can you track the real change the intervention catalyses, as well as the prospects of stabilisation and continuation of the achieved changes? As this book stresses, social change programmes have to focus on (the change in) practices, not looking solely at individual behaviours and market attributes. This chapter offers guidance on how to collect and interpret evidence in the light of social practices. This involves a workable synthesis with the already existing good traditions of evaluation.

A process of how a programme can contribute to social change is depicted in Figure 5.1. It should be read from left to right, starting with the problem analysis and the mapping of the territory the programme 'inhabits' (see Chapter 3, sections 3.1 and 3.2). Even at this early stage, it is useful to think about the specific aspects or phenomena that characterise (convey the essence of) the socio-material network that supports the problematic practice. This facilitates finding indicators for further assessment. When the objectives of the programme are laid out, coalition building (Chapter 1, section 1.2 and Chapter 3, section 3.5) and programme design usually begin, either in parallel or alternately. The initiator agrees with coalition partners on the main tools and activities of the programme and the investments they call for. The investments have to be described not only in terms of money, but also in terms of time, material, technological equipment, space, infrastructure, volunteers, know-how and relations. Intangible human resources can be translated into time and money.

The design of the programme attempts to achieve congruence and cohesion with the problematic/desired practice elements and the programme tools and measures (see Chapter 2, section 2.3 and Chapter 4, section 4.1) that help to disrupt, substitute or modify problematic practices or to create new ones (see Chapter 3, section 3.3). The activities which constitute the programme, e.g., interactive or safer things and improved environments, are called *outputs* and are reported in terms of their presence/availability for target group members. Often measurement is numerical: the number of booklets produced, workshops held, people trained etc.

The next question is how target group members engage in and respond to these interventions. What changes do they experience in terms of skills, knowledge,

---

1   Specific methodologies have been developed that connect research findings and other evidence with money (e.g., Social Return on Investment), and show social and environmental impacts of activities and projects in monetary value (http://www.thesroinetwork.org).

2   Some programme summary booklets combine quantitative evidence with narratives by beneficiaries, and include professional graphic design; see HCT group (2013); Craft Cafe (2011).

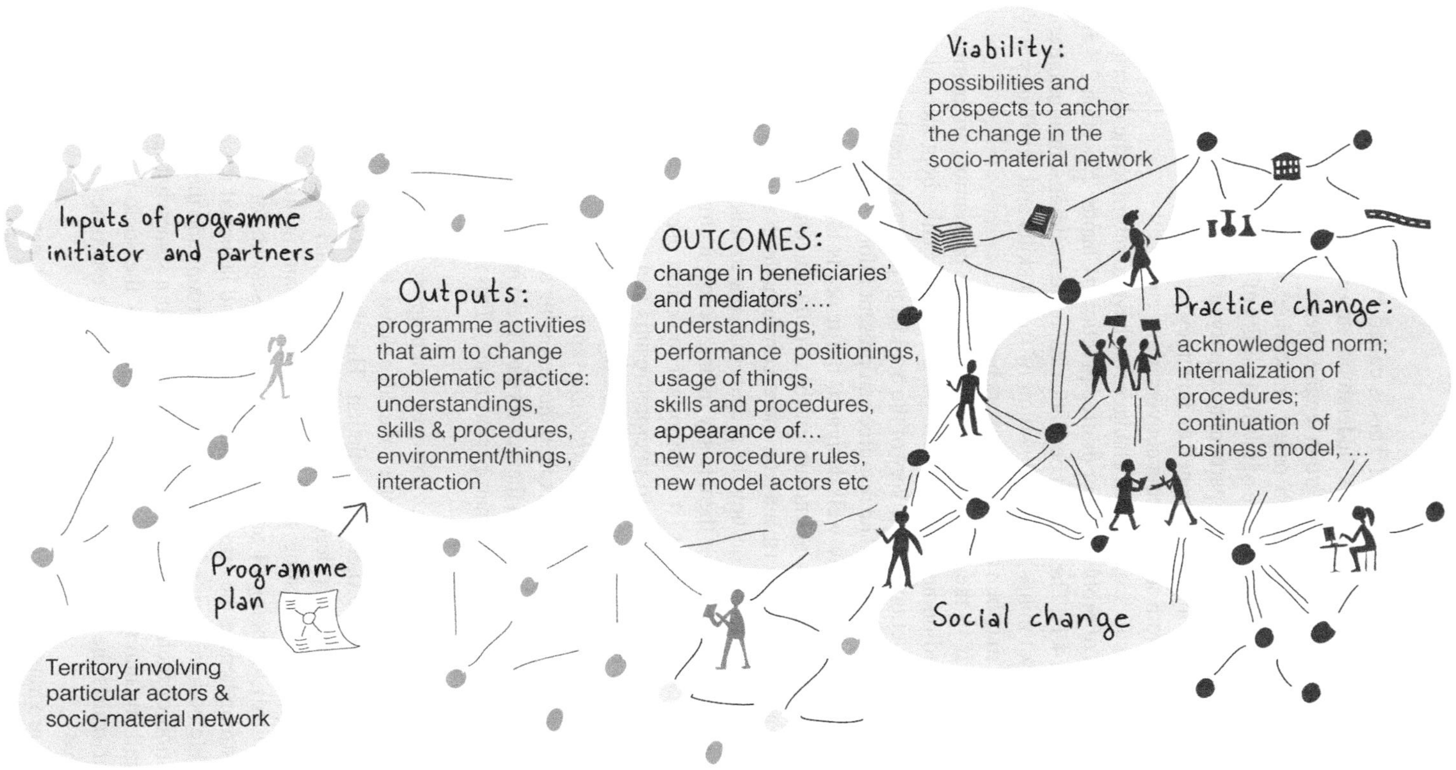
Inputs of programme initiator and partners
Outputs:
programme activities that aim to change problematic practice: understandings, skills & procedures, environment/things, interaction
OUTCOMES:
change in beneficiaries' and mediators'.... understandings, performance positionings, usage of things, skills and procedures, appearance of... new procedure rules, new model actors etc
Viability:
possibilities and prospects to anchor the change in the socio-material network
Practice change:
acknowledged norm; internalization of procedures; continuation of business model, ...
Programme plan
Social change
Territory involving particular actors & socio-material network

Figure 5.1 Information needed for evaluation in various programme stages

understanding and mutual relations? This is called evaluation of the *programme outcomes*, which are most often understood among practitioners as short-term, immediate effects. Target group engagements can be assessed by what the beneficiaries do: visiting web pages or service outlets, reading distributed information materials, being aware of the availability of services, buying delivered/sold products, spending time on a particular activity or discontinuing participation. In addition, information can be gleaned on how they perceive the programme from feedback gathered from social media conversations etc.

In order to measure experienced changes, we have to return to the description of the components of problematic or desired practices (Chapter 2, section 2.3 and Chapter 4, section 4.1). The shifts in beneficiaries' understandings, their usage and evaluation of (new) things, their acquisition of (new) skills and familiarity with (new) procedures may be valuable indicators here.

For example, if in the course of an alcohol abuse prevention programme a booklet is produced on how teachers and parents should talk about alcohol with teenagers, the production and delivery of the booklet to parents or teachers is not a sufficient marker of success. The resource can present information in an attractive way and may be graphically well designed, but it needs to convey information on how to motivate parents to embark on those difficult conversations with kids who are at a sensitive age (it may be more comfortable to think one's child is safe), as well as expertise on how to prepare parents to talk with teenagers on normative topics (it is easy for them to say 'mum, I know it already; don't worry'). In order to evaluate outcomes, it is important to collect users' feedback as well as including know-how on how to interpret results and improve the product. In order to estimate further application of the newly acquired skills and knowledge, we suggest using a *performance positioning* approach, which deals with how people discursively compare and explain their existing and possible ways of doing something (routines and habits in their everyday lives) in relation to the suggested way of doing it (i.e., a good or smart performance). This method is explained more fully in Chapter 5, section 5.3.

Estimation of outcomes is, however, incomplete if we study only the beneficiaries' immediate experience. We also have to ask how the processes will continue after the project's completion. The above-mentioned parents' anti-alcohol booklet may be a dead end if it is not augmented with other activities. Thus, for example, assisting another programme team in justifying the need for (continued) financing of an *online* counselling service for parents is a step towards strengthening the effect. Produced things and launched interactions have to be viable both in terms of their utility for target groups and their resilience: the continuation of their existence in their present or in a somewhat reshaped form (while still maintaining the initial general aim). If the socio-material network rejects or resists the change induced by programme outcomes, the change will not survive.

If the programme has reshaped the socio-material network that supported earlier unwanted practices, it is essential to ask before terminating the project how well-anchored the new network configurations are. The individual behaviour change approach assumes that well-motivated and well-prepared individuals 'anchor' the changes in the socio-material network: informed/warned consumers start to buy 'correct' products and thereby pressure producers, citizens who are equipped with self-monitoring devices start pursuing a healthier lifestyle etc. (see Chapter 2, section 2.2 and Table 2.1).

The practice-based approach pays extra attention to the *provisional stability* (e.g., Saunders, 2011) of interventions. The main way to establish stability is to co-operate with other actors in the field and build strong coalitions. Evaluation has to consider the logic of the field where the coalition partners operate (Chapter 1, section 1.2). When the main intermediary with primary target groups is a business organisation, the life of the programme depends on economic feasibility and, consequently, the socio-material network that supports the business model needs to be assessed. Programme realisability is expanded on in Chapter 3, sections 3.4 and 3.5, using the example of a university canteen offering organic meals. This case illustrates how the viability of a micro-level social change undertaken in the economic field can be measured, and how the initial plan can be transformed to anchor the change in the socio-material network. The main conclusion of this analysis was that offering one hundred per cent organic food was manageable only with continuous assistance from the change initiators. However, the plan to cook meals with some organic components having more stable supply chains was economically feasible for the canteen without additional external input.

If the initiated change is connected with policy, public legitimacy and the legal framework are important factors in viability. For example, one of the main components of Australia's governmental anti-smoking strategy was a requirement for plain cigarette packaging (see Figure 1.2)[3] and, not surprisingly, this was actively resisted by tobacco companies. In addition to lobbying and articles in mass media, tobacco companies started legal action against the Australian government in the High Court of Australia, claiming the ownership of intellectual property related to tobacco packaging and asking for compensation for profits lost due to public health advertisements (warnings) on the packs (Rimmer, 2013). The government had to defend the legality and constitutionality of the plain packaging requirement as a specific information standard for products (Rimmer, 2013). The court ruling in favour of the government was a significant milestone, yet not the only factor ensuring the viability of the intervention. Time will tell whether removing all branding and marketing elements from cigarette packs, along with such other actions as a tax increase and control of the black market, can really re-configure the socio-material network and disrupt or change smoking practices (to be discussed below), while tobacco companies continue to stir up doubts about the

---

3 In Australia, since December 2012, cigarettes have to be packaged in standardised brown packs, without any graphic brand elements, only the brand name in standard font. The brown packs are covered with visual and verbal health warnings.

packaging requirement in the media. That brings us to the much-debated concept of impact.

In addition to immediate outcomes, evidence on wider and long-term *social impact* is expected by financing institutions.[4] Outcomes and social impact are different phenomena. The former focuses on the effectiveness of programme activities' realisation, e.g., how accessible they were for the target groups. The impact is about which changes an intervention catalyses in the longer term. Chapter 2, section 2.1 briefly introduced sociological explanations of how social changes occur and charted various ways life politics is exercised. What constitutes long-term social change depends on how its mechanisms are envisaged: either as a shift in individuals' understandings of the social good and their empowerment to employ and change rules and resources, or a transformation in the structural frameworks that are supposed to determine actors' behaviours. In the first case, more emphasis is placed on tracking individuals' opinions, knowledge, skills and relationships through surveys, focus-groups, tests etc. In the second case, structural changes are measured by statistics, document analysis, expert opinions, observations, and testing access to services and products. The Business Dictionary defines 'Social impact' (n.d.) as an 'effect of an activity on the social fabric of a community and the well-being of individuals and families' and the respective analysis as 'the measurement and assessment of the social impact created by not-for-profit, for profit, or public sector organisations or programs'.[5] This definition is compatible with the social practice approach, as it stresses the collective and socio-cultural nature (the *social fabric of a community*) of the expected change and leads to a search for evidence regarding social structure and relations. It also sees well-being as a(n) (independent) gauge, leaving it open as to whether it should be appraised on the expert level (according to certain criteria) or as a subjective self-assessment (the latter being the conceptual basis of happiness studies).

In the framework of the present book, proof of practice change could be that a certain way of doing something is acknowledged as a group norm that is considered to be personally applicable (more details in Chapter 5, section 5.3.), when key actors (e.g., the management board of an organisation or the staff of a service provider) have accepted and internalised particular procedures, when a social enterprise continues to operate etc. Evaluating impact is always tricky, because no programme provider operates in a vacuum and many phenomena emerge in parallel. One has to be especially careful when measuring returns on investments, because in other conditions the same intervention may be financially or socially less/more profitable, as circumstances and contexts for inputs may vary. Thus it becomes a contested issue as to how much and what exactly can be attributed to a particular programme. We can speak of social change when the problem indicators

---

4   Medium-term outcomes and longer-term outcomes are also used in evaluation models (e.g., Weiss, 1972), more or less in the same sense.

5   The same term is also used by social enterprises and analysts, such as the International Social Impact Analysts Association (http://www.siaassociation.org/).

show a trend towards decreasing and when the socio-material network enabling particular practices has been transformed. Even though the 'net' effect of one particular intervention may be sociologically very complicated or even dubious to assess, it is inevitable that a programme's contribution to a favourable end has to be demonstrated to funders, as well as to the public. This rather challenging endeavour is further explained below.

5.2 The problems of assessing social impact

Social impact assessment is a widely discussed topic: there are numerous handbooks and learning resources available (see 'Further reading'). Advisers insist on collecting compelling evidence from sensibly chosen parallel cases (with and without intervention) and, ideally, implementing an experimental design (see e.g., Hornsby, 2012). Academia is more sceptical about supporting practitioners' experimental design, because of 'daunting methodological problems in identifying robust causal links between interventions, programmes and policies and desired outcomes' (Saunders, 2011, p. 89). Despite funders' eagerness to determine causality and make sure positive effects can be credited to a particular source with certainty, it is very expensive and in a sense misleading to give very definitive answers here because of the complex nature of social problems and contexts. Some disciplinary associations (such as the European Evaluation Society) have approved more open, multiple-method approaches, admitting that evaluating effects is complicated, particularly in multidimensional interventions that require the application of a variety of different methods, both qualitative and quantitative (Saunders et al., 2011). Such means as constructing narratives of reasonable causal chains (Wolff and Schönherr, 2011), expert evaluations, contribution analysis (Mayne, 2001) and counter-factual analysis (Mark and Henry, 2006) have been recommended.

Critics also ask whether proof of long-term social impact should be required from all mission-driven organisations. Large international funds measure immediate outputs (e.g., mosquito nets delivered) and outcomes (e.g., participants' feedback about a course) and interpret the results on the basis of correlations between two factors (e.g., nets and malaria cases, or test results after the course and high school attendance) taken from other projects' reports, in order to evaluate possible future effects (Ebrahim, 2013). The reason for doing so is pragmatic: assessment is complex and expensive.

Being realistic in (not) asking programme implementers to measure impact is essential: 'It requires a level of research expertise, commitment to longitudinal study, and allocation of resources that are typically beyond the capabilities of implementing organizations. It is crucial to identify when it makes sense to measure impacts and when it might be best to stick with outputs – especially when an organization's control over results is limited, and causality remains poorly understood' (Ebrahim, 2013). We partly agree with that statement. Methods used in academic research on practice change – comparative analysis of test samples (e.g., Nyborg and Røpke, 2013), years-long ethnography (e.g., Majchrzak et al., 2012), and historical research of statistical databases (e.g., Tomlinson and McMeekin, 2001) – are often not accessible to social change programme makers due to temporal and financial constraints or insufficiency of methodological knowledge and skills.

As a possible solution, we suggest a pragmatic, practice-based approach that examines the programme's possible long-term impact as a combination of outcomes, viability and positive contributing effects of factors outside the programme. Viability depends on the existing socio-material network and actors' support in enabling the desired processes, e.g. new or reformed (organisational) policies, new (or newly trained) people, new (or re-organised) spaces and new resources (things and know-how). These indicators show how the socio-material network that practices are embedded in is shaped in order to enable self-reproduction of the desired practice.

Social change reveals itself in new or modified routinised behaviours, e.g., consumption, education, industry, commerce or health activity patterns. To track any changes, some measurement should be made before the programme starts, followed by assessment after and, if possible, in the middle of the programme. If a 'before' and 'after' comparison is not feasible, research on comparative sites may be considered ensuring, as much as possible, comparability in terms of time, treatment etc. Real life processes involve many more contributing factors than laboratory tests or random trials. Thus, at best, it is the programme's positive contribution (but rarely a single causality) that can be shown through these measurements. Evaluators propose 'alignment rather than attribution' by scrutinising what indicates the contribution of a particular intervention, and they adhere to the 'indicative rather than definitive principle' (Saunders, 2011, p. 99).

For example, in their struggle against plain cigarette packaging in Australia, tobacco companies argued that a reduction in market volume had been caused primarily by the tax increase, not the packaging reform. Legislators objected to these claims by producing empirical evidence of the combined effect of plain packaging and warning labels on attractiveness and taste expectations (Cancer Council Victoria, 2011) and survey findings on the stable or decreasing numbers of buyers of very low-cost and smuggled cigarettes (Scollo et al., 2014). In real life, various aspects – price, social norms and feelings associated with the packaging – combine, and the effect on smoking habits develops over time, as public norms change slowly and the issue is still extensively discussed because of the active lobbying and media advocacy from both sides. To sum up, any determination of which factor has had the greatest impact is speculative and preliminary, because in reality they are all connected. This is stressed by researchers, for example, Paul Harrison says: 'One of the real mistakes public health can make is to over-emphasise the effects of a single factor because if it is small or changes, it then gives the tobacco industry something to come back with, in terms of pedalling [*sic*] their own studies' (Jackson-Webb, 2014).

Table 5.1   Main categories used in programme evaluation

Concept	Application in the case of tobacco prevention
Input	Production of warning signs, modifications in pricing and taxing politics and prohibitions on smoking in public spaces
Output	Availability of lower-nicotine cigarettes, warning labels on packs, fewer shops, less overt cigarette advertising in public spaces, (anti-tobacco) media publicity, and law suits against tobacco companies
Outcome = short-term outcome	Change in cigarette buying: diminishing brand loyalty, preference for cheaper products, decrease in total and public smoking and its acceptability
Programme viability	Lawsuits of tobacco companies fail to derail the anti-tobacco policy actions, public support groups and social media campaign for stricter anti-smoking policy, and organisations and groups adopt smoke-free behaviour in their social routines
Social impact = long-term outcome	Fewer young people begin smoking, more smokers quit or plan to quit, decrease in cancer incidents among smokers, and fewer spaces for smoking
Contributing effects (of outside factors)	Religious affiliations that support giving up smoking, and low availability of alternative tobacco products
Side-effects	Larger black market of tobacco products, protest culture among smokers, worsening organisational relations due to the disappearance of public smoking rooms, and weight increase among those who quit smoking

Saunders (2011) proposes using the 'courtroom' instead of the 'laboratory' metaphor, which aptly suits the Australian case (tobacco companies' litigation); courtroom-like evaluations 'aggregate available knowledge of a circumstance and induce what might have caused it' (p. 99). Mayne (2001) has proposed *contribution analysis*, in which various explanations of a condition are contemplated. It is not always easy to determine exact contribution, especially when different indicators are contradictory. In the above case, tobacco companies and health officials used different evidence in their argumentation about the influence of plain packaging on smoking (volume of cigarettes sold, total household expenditure on tobacco and cigarettes, calls to hot-lines by smokers who wanted to quit, and survey and experimental data). A positive contribution can be evaluated by weighing different types of indicators and building chains, though this process is not mechanical.

Programmes operate in a multifaceted social reality in constant flux, investing (evaluation) efforts in programme *viability*, and the resilience of its outcomes might be a more appropriate measurement than trying to evaluate overall social impact. In practical terms, it is not so much a question of the 'pure' relationship between the programme and the changed pattern of a particular practice, but whether the supporting socio-material network persists, tightens or loosens.

Supporting networks may be both local and international. For example, the plain packaging effort can be associated with shifts in the Australian smoking situation. It is internationally widely discussed that some countries, including France, are contemplating similar measures on plain packaging of some foodstuffs (BBC Europe, 2014).

Overall, we suggest appraising social impact by also referring to similar cases in other sites and by envisaging the place of the programme in a wider context of various drivers pushing in the same direction. Seeking professional help in calculating the financial appropriateness and social value of programmes is in some cases highly recommended. Table 5.1 sums up the main relevant terms and gives brief examples of their interpretation.

In the last section, we give some methodological advice on how to actually conduct evaluation.

5.3 Stages and methods of programme evaluation

Figure 5.2 provides a visual synopsis of the argument below. The selection of *indicators* is a crucial part of every evaluation. Good indicators reveal logical, meaningful chains between the components of particular phenomena over time, and they are sensitive to change but not too volatile under repeated measurements (this proves that other factors not measured influence the indicator more). Murray Saunders (2011) elaborates on three modes of indicators. The first are areas, activities, domains or phenomena on which evidence will be collected (e.g., possible domains showing smoking reduction can be measured as a general share of smokers, the number of young people who just started smoking, the proportion of people who are thinking about quitting etc.). The second mode is about the existence of new practices (e.g., sale of low-alcohol wines and beers). The third mode is the predefined or prescribed state to be achieved (e.g., ensuring fire safety in the home: batteries for smoke detectors, electrical equipment, and fireproof candle holders as a part of fire safety practices).

Some evaluation may be planned before the programme commences, but it is not necessary in the following cases: the baseline is well-known (as was the case in the university canteen discussed in Chapter 3, sections 3.4 and 3.5), information exists from earlier research, and when there is a similar, comparable group or site where there was no intervention (referred to as a 'control' group or site in experimental studies). If 'before–after' juxtapositions are planned, the state of affairs has to be identified before programme activities are launched (see the left side of Figure 5.2).

Typical research questions to be posed at an early stage are: what are the current practices of target groups? How can the things, material environment, skills, knowledge and meanings of the problematic practices be described? Subsequent comparability has to be kept in mind and, as much as possible, situations and key actors should be selected who are likely to be accessible after the programme.

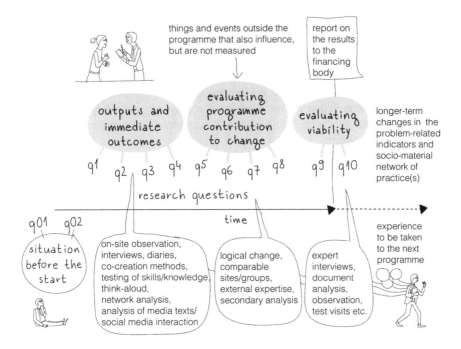

Figure 5.2   Stages and methods of programme evaluation

It is not mandatory to assemble a panel of informants, because in research on practices carried out by actors it is not necessary to involve exactly the same people, since the focus is on the ways practices are enacted in particular settings. But, if panel research is easy (e.g., there are agreements with people to participate again), evaluation can rely on that as well. If indicators (e.g., about a new practice) aren't available, this needs to be dealt with. Methods for gathering evidence before the programme launch are numerous, depending on the particular field of activity, type of change and target group. References to guidebooks on social research are given at the end of the chapter.

We suggest documenting the current state according to elements of practice: skills/procedures, meanings, things and environments, and interaction. *Knowledge* and *skills*, use of *things*, *space* and *infrastructure* can sometimes be tested (e.g., informants are asked to find particular information on a web page) or inquired about in terms of self-evaluation, but in the case of bodily practices it may be worthwhile to arrange a series of observations (e.g., of parents shopping with children). Also, the 'think-aloud' method can be helpful (e.g., letting patients navigate a new counselling website, and encouraging them to express out loud all the impressions and associations evoked by the website). Various tests using sensors, such as neuromarketing (Genco et al., 2013), are also popular. In this case, co-operation with scientists or a research firm is needed.

Meanings ascribed to particular activities can be collected by asking for (dis) agreement with verbal statements about existing norms, and by using visual stimuli. Qualitative analysis, which interprets subjects' non-standardised verbal self-expression (gathered via interviews or from self-produced texts, photos etc.), is very valuable, because it may reveal nuances (e.g., about the emergence of the new practice) that do not surface in surveys. It is sensible to combine qualitative measures with standardised, quantitative measurements to get a comprehensive picture.

After the launch of a programme, its development has to be monitored. As mentioned above, both beneficiaries and intermediaries need to be included. When market actors are involved, viability evaluation needs to be sensitive to their field of activity (see Chapter 1, section 1.2) and operational logic (see the case of the university canteen in Chapter 3, sections 3.4 and 3.5). If the interventions interfere too much with organisational routines and mechanisms, provisional stability and efficient performance will be negatively impacted. Workable methods here are observations (see e.g., McDonald, 2005; Patton, 2002), mystery shopping (Stucker, 2006), informal interviews or conversations with staff members, and inquiries about business results.

The next step is to examine the intervention's contribution to *practice change* (see Figure 5.1). As mentioned in the previous section, *practice change* is influenced by the interaction of a number of things and events. It is important to carefully follow and document new significant events, and phenomena that occur during the programme, as they may add to the effect. What is relevant should be determined based on the programme team's expertise. We suggest using the same set of indicators – data collected through various methods, such as standardised or in-depth interviews, observations and diary research – before and after the intervention. For example, the authors of this book conducted a study on how low-income families coped with the switch-over to the euro and price increases that accompanied it by asking informants to keep shopping diaries (with space for free comments) and conducting in-depth interviews with them (Keller and Vihalemm, 2015). Interviews carried out in homes were complemented with observation (e.g., how informants used gadgets for calculating between the euro and the national currency). Here remarkable changes in skills (calculating and budgeting), in relation to things (coins and notes vs bank cards) emerged. Shopping diaries revealed that actual shopping habits did not change that much. This combination of methods provided a multi-layered picture of how the reform had affected everyday life.

Another way to investigate the change is the (change in) key actor *performance positionings* (Keller and Halkier, 2014). Positioning (Harré and van Langenhove, 1999) represents a particular kind of situational fixation of social interaction, with a focus on normative content and negotiation in interactions. Studying performance positionings draws on qualitative text analysis, focusing on informants' sayings about the existing and possible ways of doing something: using things, moving through spaces, interacting with others etc., in relation to the (normative) suggestion given in the programme.

We propose a framework for analysis that makes it possible to trace positioning along two axes: (a) *change vs maintenance* of existing practices and (b) *coherence vs incoherence* of changes in practice elements (do all elements change, and in what direction?). An empirical study undertaken before and after Estonia privatised its electricity market revealed that the elements of practices such as understandings (electricity packages and stock prices), procedures and skills (comparison of prices in the special web portal), and engagements (dedication to budget management or to price screening) did not always move in one clear direction. The most 'fluctuating' were cases where practice elements (meanings, skills and things) were contradictory: clients switched electricity packages several times and their general attitudes towards the possibilities of smart consumption and the empowerment of consumers were very pessimistic (Vihalemm and Keller, 2013). Methodologically, we suggest that the analysis of diaries and interview discourse works quite well in analysing practice change when more time-consuming and expensive ethnographic methods such as (participant) observations are not available.

Practice change can also be indicated when a certain way of doing something is acknowledged as a personally applicable and 'do-able' group norm. For example, when a campaign is launched with a concrete call-to-action to keep drunk friends from going swimming, programme initiators may ask target group members whether (a) the habit of monitoring the activities of friends at a party is normal in their peer groups and (b) if preventing them from going into the water would be acceptable in their circles. In Estonia, where this issue has been dealt with for three years in awareness campaigns, trainings and point-of-practice communication (see Chapter 2, section 2.2), studies have shown that after the campaign the informants reported less frequently that keeping an eye on each other at parties was common in their friendship circles. Informants also reported less frequently that they didn't keep an eye on each other. Instead, the share of 'do not know' answers increased. We interpret this result as growing self-reflection: the young men became less optimistic about how safe their partying practices actually were. At the same time, the assessment of the acceptability of intervening (i.e., obstructing a friend) was steadily positive (Trink, 2015). People in this condition are generally more open to developing new skills and habits when supported by relevant communication, which can be enhanced by clever products. Other campaigns, such as keeping friends from driving when drunk, can support the formation of the 'keeping an eye on' habit as part of partying practices. However, willingness to intervene in one particular 'seasonal' danger may not have enough power to establish a general monitoring habit.

Shifts in interactions and communication networks can also be illuminating. Relevant issues include the existence of people who can be asked for help, participation in community activities, public meetings and social media conversations, (online) mutual advice, volunteer work and media advocacy. In the case of (online) communities, methods that visualise relationships, such as network analysis (see e.g., Hanneman and Riddle, 2011), can be employed, as well as qualitative content analysis (see e.g., Ezzy, 2002) of forum or social media postings. Finally, various interviews with experts (teachers, scientists or other relevant stakeholders) can provide invaluable data.

Numerous research methods and strategies are available, each having its own strengths and weaknesses. It is always more productive to combine them. However, programme evaluation has to fit within the parameters of project funding and available time. We suggest co-operating with universities, where both researchers and students conduct studies. It can be a win–win situation when students get a 'piece of reality' to investigate and a programme team receives systematic analysis. Since this chapter cannot give detailed methodological instructions, the reader will need to consult methods handbooks, of which there is an impressive abundance. Some of the authors' favourites are listed in 'Further reading'.

5.4 Summary

Proceeding from the overall conceptual basis of this book, we stress a focus on (change in) practices, and not depending on only individual behaviours or market attributes in programme evaluation. Since evaluation is a multi-layered and established complex of different traditions, it is sensible to seek a workable, yet informative and reliable combination of methods. In doing this, it is necessary to distinguish between programme outcomes, most often understood as short-term, immediate effects, and social impact, which is a longer term change in the social well-being of people. Measuring the latter is very tricky and attributing causality here must be done with extreme caution because in a social situation many phenomena intersect and overlap; clinically dissecting single causal links may not be prudent. Instead, we outline more open, multiple-method approaches that examine a programme's possible long-term impact as a combination of outcomes, viability and positive contributing effects of factors outside the programme. This can be done by weighing different types of indicators, comparing 'before' and 'after' states, as well as different sites before and after the respective interventions, and building chains, though not mechanically. Both positive and negative side-effects have to be considered.

The basic elements of social practices can serve as an analysis framework: skills/procedures, meanings, things and environments, and social interaction need to be documented before and after the beginning of the programme, using accessible and suitable analysis methods. Thus we do not advocate an experimental design to appraise 'pure' causality, because social life includes numerous different factors and influences, whose effects may be ambivalent and contradictory. Both the perspective of the programme key actors and changes in the socio-material network have to be examined because the overall impact (if there is any) emerges from a complex interaction of these factors.

Measurement of programme effects in some form is mandatory in most cases, especially due to funders' expectations. To do this professionally, skilled help from relevant consulting companies, research institutes and universities has to be sought because adequate research and evaluation expertise is the foundation of convincing and communicable assessments. The relevant stakeholders have the right to know how well the interventions have fared, which paves the way for support for and funding of future programmes.

Further reading

Web resources on evaluation

Better Evaluation (n.d.) Better evaluation. Resources. Retrieved from http://betterevaluation.org/resources
Craft Café (2011, August). Creative solutions to isolation and loneliness. Social return on investment evaluation. Summary report. Retrieved from http://www.impactarts.co.uk/files/Craft%20Cafe%20SROI%20Summary.pdf
Foundation Centre (n.d.). Tools and resources for assessing social impact database. Retrieved from http://trasi.foundationcenter.org/
HCT group (2013). Impact report 2013. Growing enterprise, growing impact. Retrieved from http://hctgroup.org/uploaded/hct-group-impact-report-2013.pdf
Innovation Network (n.d.). Logic model workbook. Retrieved from http://www.innonet.org/client_docs/File/logic_model_workbook.pdf
Inspiring Impact (n.d.). Impact hub. Retrieved from http://inspiringimpact.org/listings
Social Impact Analysts Association (n.d.). Resources centre. Retrieved from http://www.siaassociation.org/resources/
The Global Value Exchange (n.d.). The webpage of the Global Value Exchange. Retrieved from http://globalvaluexchange.org
The SROI Network (n.d.). The webpage of the SROI Network. Retrieved from http://www.thesroinetwork.org

Methods overviews

Berger, A.A. (2011). *Media and communication research: An introduction to qualitative and quantitative approaches*. Thousand Oaks, CA: Sage.
Daymon, C. and Holloway, I. (2011). *Qualitative research methods in public relations and marketing communications* (2nd ed.). New York, NY: Routledge.
Ezzy, D. (2002). *Qualitative analysis: Practice and innovation*. New South Wales, Australia: Allen and Unwin.
Flick, U. (2009). *An introduction to qualitative research* (4th ed.). London, England: Sage.

Hanneman, R., and Riddle, M. (2005). *Introduction to social network methods*. Retrieved from http://faculty.ucr.edu/~hanneman/nettext/

Kozinets, R.V. (2010). *Netnography: Doing ethnographic research online*. London, England: Sage.

Sage (n.d.). Sage research methods. The essential online tool for researchers product (accessible via libraries, with access permit). Retrieved from http://www.sagepub.com/aboutSRMO.sp

Chapter 6

Programme design tool-kit

The last part of this book presents the gist of our whole argument according to programme design stages. It is captured in Figure 6.1. The bullet points below provide additional substance to the stages. In most cases, references are given to the sections(s) where the respective topic is treated in detail.

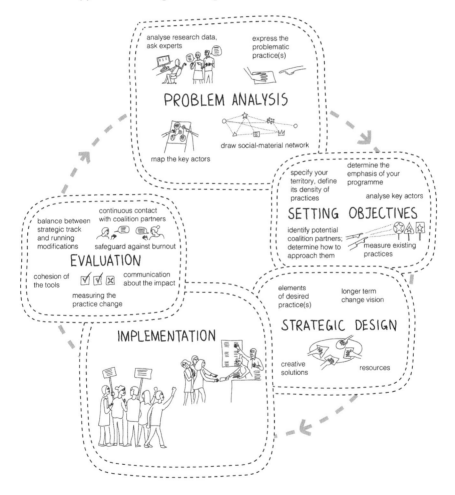

Figure 6.1   Programme design stages

Problem analysis

- Usually ideas for social change proposals are formulated while preparing to write funding proposals. The invisible hand of a funding programme plays a role as a guide to success. The description of a funding programme is meant to inform applicants of its opportunities, but it is usually taken as a guideline to get money. Try to step off this treadmill and ask yourself and your team what sort of social problem you are actually going to tackle (and remember that you probably will not solve it entirely).
- Analyse research evidence relevant to the problem and ask for expert opinions.
- Express the problem in the language of everyday practices: what is it that people do that is detrimental to achieving a wider social good (see Chapter 3, section 3.1)? Avoid buzzwords from funding programmes.
- At this stage, stick to the big issues and big picture, even though the entire problem cannot – in most cases – be eliminated by one programme.
- Analyse the most relevant problematic practices according to their elements: meanings, skills and material environment, as well as the social interaction that binds them together (see section 3.2).
- Draw the socio-material network with nodes and provisionally delineate your territory (see Figure 3.4).
- Map the key actors (target groups, stakeholders and potential coalition partners) in your provisional territory (see sections 3.1 and 3.2).
- Sketch the map of your territory and paste it on your wall for further comments and criticism.
- Use action research and co-creation with programme beneficiaries.
- Talk to project managers, volunteers etc. who have worked on the same problem and/or the same target group. Discuss the conclusions and controversies you have found in the research.
- Get embodied experience, go feel the space and environment, perform activities, talk to the people (face-to-face and in social media networks), and look at photographs of the everyday environment. Involve your team in this activity, as your words will not be enough to provide a clear picture.

Objective setting

- Specify your territory and define the density of the practices you are going to intervene in (see section 3.2 and Figure 3.7). The overall practice change goal is bound to be quite big, yet a concrete programme requires understandable and adequate problem setting, a point of departure and a distinct (even though open-ended) territory: a clear location and site, target groups and a distinction between the short-term (what can be done within a project or programme) and the long-term vision (what the real practice change is aimed at).

- Decide on the emphasis of your intervention: creating new practices, modifying existing ones, replacing one practice with another or a complete rupture, where you aim to do away with a (set of) practice(s) (see section 3.3).
- Analyse the key actors according to their capacity and the breadth of the social change (see section 3.4, Figures 3.11 and 3.14).
- Identify potential coalition partners by using the problematic practice as your starting point (see section 3.5 and Figures 3.11, 3.13 and 3.15).
- Think about how to approach the partners you want to engage and determine their interests; probe for their capacity and willingness for long-term collaboration (see Chapter 1, section 1.2 and Chapter 3, section 3.5).
- Take some time to start designing programme evaluation. If 'before' and 'after' are important milestones, the existing (problematic) practices prior to the programme need to be analysed and documented for future benchmarking (see Chapter 5, section 5.2). Take a fresh look at the sketch on your wall, and check whether the description of 'before' describes the practice holistically.
- It is normal to encounter different shapes and sizes of challenges on your way. One of the potential pitfalls is slipping back into the individualist 'raise awareness' paradigm. Try your best to avoid this! Also, institutional documents and thinking patterns are rife with bureaucratic jargon which expresses 'world improvement' in abstract phrases of reducing or increasing something, combating something. Treat such formulations as the macro level background and long-term vision, but they cannot serve as your micro- or meso-level programme objectives, or as warning phrases in public communication.

Strategic design

- Determine the elements of the desired practices, and compare them with the elements of problematic practices that you identified earlier (see Chapter 3, section 3.2 and all of Chapter 4).
- Use these elements as your guiding lights when selecting methods, 'treatments', interventions and activities as building blocks of your programme (see Chapter 4, section 4.1 and Figure 4.1).
- Back-casting is one way to plot a sequence of activities and events: what has to be done in order to achieve long-term practice change? Which concrete steps need to be taken?
- Initiate creative solutions by using different methods and involving local knowledge as much as possible (e.g., crowd-sourcing and co-creation). For

a possible selection of how to affect meanings, materials/things and skills, see Chapter 4, sections 4.2–4.4.

- Combine the activities of your coalition partners into a cohesive whole, and divide the labour. Check whether you have the partners needed to cover the building blocks of the programme entirely.
- Analyse ideas critically according to your resources, and finalise your strategy and tactical plan.
- Analyse the coalition partners' interests and concerns: what is the common ground and capability of accommodating potentially conflicting or diverging paths?
- Be pragmatic in communicating and negotiating with your coalition partners.
- If possible, try to live and experience first-hand what you want your target groups to do. Is the new normality habitable?

Implementation and evaluation

- Navigate the balance between your strategic track and a constant need to adjust and modify your programme along the way due to outside pressure, shifting circumstances or unforeseen events. Decide what the core of your mission is, i.e., what you cannot let go of even if your programme is on the verge of capsizing (see Chapter 4, section 4.6), and where there is room to manoeuvre.
- Call your partners, ask how they are doing, and ask whether you can help.
- Organise informal get-togethers with your team. These normally take extra working hours, but show your team that they are as important as the programme. Switching between topics of discussion also takes time, but helps a team to loosen up and take a fresh look at wicked problems (see Chapter 3, section 3.1).
- Monitor the cohesion of the tools and methods according to the logic of the desired practice, the outcomes and viability of the programme (see Chapter 5, sections 5.1 and 5.2).
- If possible, study the developing practice change during the programme (see sections 5.2 and 5.3).
- Keep a diary during the programme for further projects.
- Be creative in evaluating the contributing effects of your project and outside factors, consult experts and use multiple methods. Beware of confusing contributing effects and outputs with social impact (see section 5.2).
- Compile, or commission from an expert, an analysis of the resilience of the new practices and the sustainability of the new normality.
- Re-draw the sketch on your wall, and congratulate your team.

References

Ajzen, I. (1985). From intentions to actions: A theory of planned behavior. In J. Kuhl and J. Beckman (eds), *Action-control: From cognition to behavior* (pp. 11–39). Heidelberg, Germany: Springer.

Alemanno, A. and Garde, A. (2013). The emergence of an EU lifestyle policy: The case of alcohol, tobacco and unhealthy diets. *Common Market Law Review* 50, 1745–86. Retrieved from http://www.kluwerlawonline.com/abstract.php?area=Journals&id=COLA2013165

Anderson, C. (2005, April 26). What's the difference between policies and procedures? Retrieved from http://www.bizmanualz.com/blog/whats-the-difference-between-policies-and-procedures.html

Andreasen, A.R. (1995). *Marketing social change: Changing behavior to promote health, social development, and the environment.* San Fransisco, CA: Jossey-Bass.

Andreasen, A.R. (2003). *Strategic marketing for nonprofit organizations.* Englewood Cliffs, NJ: Prentice-Hall.

Archer, M.S. (1995). *Realist social theory: The morphogenetic approach.* Cambridge, England: Cambridge University Press.

Archer, M.S. (2012). *The reflexive imperative in late modernity.* Cambridge, England: Cambridge University Press.

Arusaar-Tamming, K. (2007). 1985. Aasta nõukogude alkoholipoliitika ja selle tagajärjed Eesti NSVs [Soviet alcohol policy in 1985 and its effects in Estonian SSR]. *Mäetagused* 36, 35–58. doi: 10.7592./MT2007.36.arusaar

Ashcraft, K.L., Kuhn, T.R. and Cooren, F. (2009). Constitutional amendments: Materializing organizational communication. *Academy of Management Annals* 3, 1–64. doi:10.1080/19416520903047186

Atkinson, A. and Messy, F.-A. (2012). Measuring financial literacy: Results of the OECD / International Network on Financial Education (INFE) pilot study. *OECD Working Papers on Finance, Insurance and Private Pensions* 15, 1–73. doi:10.1787/5k9csfs90fr4-en

Barbeau, E.M., Gelder, G., Ahmed, S., Mantuefel, V. and Balbach, E.D. (2005). From strange bedfellows to natural allies: The shifting allegiance of fire service organizations in the push for federal FSC legislation. *Tobacco Control* 14, 338–45. doi:10.1136/tc.2004.010637

Bartiaux, F. and Salmon, L.R. (2012). Are there domino effects between consumers' ordinary and 'green' practices? An analysis of quantitative data from a sensitisation campaign on personal carbon footprint. *International*

Review of Sociology: Revue Internationale de Sociologie 22, 471–91. doi:10. 1080/03906701.2012.730825

Bartoletti, R. (2013, August 29). Enclosed cultures: Vegetable gardens and potential changes in consumer culture [Conference paper]. Retrieved from http:// www.researchgate.net/profile/Roberta_Bartoletti/publication/257331498_ Enclosed_cultures_vegetable_gardens_and_potential_changes_in_consumer_ culture/links/00b7d524edfafcb0b6000000?origin=publication_detail

BBC Europe (2014, September, 25). France to introduce plain cigarette packaging. Retrieved from http://www.bbc.com/news/world-europe-29367253

Beard, C. and Wilson, J. (2013). *Experiential learning: A best practice handbook for trainers and educators* (3rd ed.). London, England: Kogan Page.

Beautement, P. and Broenner, C. (2011). *Complexity demystified: A guide for practitioners.* Axminster, England: Triarchy Press.

Beck, U. (1992). *Risk society: Towards a new modernity.* New Delhi, India: Sage.

Berger, A.A. (2011). *Media and communication research: An introduction to qualitative and quantitative approaches.* Thousand Oaks, CA: Sage.

Bertilsson, M. (1984). The theory of structuration: Prospects and problems. *Acta Sociologica* 27, 339–53. doi:10.1177/000169938402700404

Better Evaluation (n.d.). Resources. Retrieved from http://betterevaluation.org/ resources

Blocker, J.S. (2006). Did prohibition really work? Alcohol prohibition as a public health innovation. *American Journal of Public Health* 96, 233–43. doi:10.2105/ AJPH.2005.065409

Blocker, J.S., Fahey, D.M. and Tyrrell, I.R. (eds) (2003). *Alcohol and temperance in modern history. A global encyclopedia.* Santa Barbara, CA: ABC-Clio.

Boston Public Library (2013, January 23). The pet, cigarette tobacco [Digital image]. Retrieved from http://bit.ly/1OYNeXP

Bourdieu, P. (1972/1977). *Outline of a theory of practice* (R. Nice, Trans.). Cambridge, England: Cambridge University Press.

Bourdieu, P. (1989). Social space and symbolic power. *Sociological Theory* 7, 14–25. Retrieved from http://www.soc.ucsb.edu/ct/pages/JWM/Syllabi/Bourd ieu/SocSpaceSPowr.pdf

Brabant, M. (2014). Have the Danes cracked childhood obesity? *BBC News.* Retrieved from http://www.bbc.com/news/health-29755469

British National Health Service (n.d.). 5 a day. Retrieved from http://www.nhs.uk/ livewell/5aday

Buckley, J. and Tuama, S.O. (2010). I send the wife to the doctor – men's behaviour as health consumers. *International Journal of Consumer Studies* 34, 587–95. doi:10.1111/j.1470-6431.2010.00908.x

Bureau of European Policy Advisers (2011). Empowering people, driving change. Social innovation in the European Union. Retrieved from http://ec.europa.eu/ bepa/pdf/publications_pdf/social_innovation.pdf

Cancer Council Victoria (2011). Plain packaging of tobacco products: A review of the evidence. Retrieved from http://www.cancer.org.au/content/pdf/Cancer

ControlPolicy/PositionStatements/TCUCCVBkgrndResrchPlainPak270511 ReEnd_FINAL_May27.pdf

Caravita, S.C.S., DiBlasio, P. and Salmivalli, C. (2008). Unique and interactive effects of empathy and social status on involvement in bullying. *Social Development* 18, 140–63. doi:10.1111/j.1467-9507.2008.00465.x

Cauchi, S. (2013, February 14). No dumb luck: Metro claims safety success. Retrieved from http://www.theage.com.au/victoria/no-dumb-luck-metro-claims-safety-success-20130214-2eelt.html

Choudry, A. and Shragge, E. (2011). Disciplining dissent: NGOs and community organizations. *Globalizations* 8, 503–17. doi:10.1080/14747731.2011.585855

Christensen, T.H. and Røpke, I. (2010). Can practice theory inspire studies of ICTs in everyday life. In B. Bräucher and J. Postill (eds), *Theorising media and practice* (pp. 233–56). New York, NY: Berghahn Books.

Cillessen, A.H. and Borch, C. (2006). Developmental trajectories of adolescent popularity: A growth curve modelling analysis. *Journal of Adolescence* 29, 935–59. doi:10.1016/j.adolescence.2006.05.005

Consumer Classroom (n.d.). What is consumer education? Retrieved from http://www.consumerclassroom.eu/about/what-is-consumer-education

Cook, G. (2001). *The discourse of advertising* (2nd ed.). London, England: Routledge.

Cooren, F., Kuhn, T.R., Cornelissen, J.P. and Clark, T. (2011). Communication, organizing, and organization: An overview and introduction to the special issue. *Organization Studies* 32, 1149–70. doi:10.1177/0170840611410836

Cornelissen, J. (2008). *Corporate communication: A guide to theory and practice* (2nd ed.). London, England: Sage.

Craft Café (2011, August). Creative solutions to isolation and loneliness. Social return on investment evaluation. Summary report. Retrieved from http://www.impactarts.co.uk/files/Craft%20Cafe%20SROI%20Summary.pdf

Cunningham, C., Cunningham, L., Ratcliffe, J. and Vaillancourt, T. (2010). A qualitative analysis of the bullying prevention and intervention recommendations of students in grades 5 to 8. *Journal of School Violence* 9, 321–38. doi:10.108 0/15388220.2010.507146

Darnton, A. and Horne, J. (2013) Influencing behaviours. Moving beyond the individual. A guide to the ISM tool. The Scottish Government. Edinburgh. Retrieved from http://www.scotland.gov.uk/Publications/2013/06/8511/down loads.

Daymon, C. and Holloway, I. (2011). *Qualitative research methods in public relations and marketing communications* (2nd ed.). New York, NY: Routledge.

Department for Children, Schools and Families, Department for Culture, Media and Sport. (2009). The impact of the commercial world on children's wellbeing. Report of an independent assessment. Retrieved from https://www.education. gov.uk/publications/eOrderingDownload/00669-2009DOM-EN.pdf

Design Thinking for Educators (n.d.). Webpage introducing the design thinking for educators. Retrieved from http://www.designthinkingforeducators.com/

Directive 2014/40/EU of the European Parliament and of the Council of 3 April 2014 on the approximation of the laws, regulations and administrative provisions of the Member States concerning the manufacture, presentation and sale of tobacco and related products and repealing Directive 2001/37/EC [2014] OJ L127/1

Ditch the Label Anti-Bullying Charity (2014). The annual bullying survey 2014. Retrieved from http://ditchthelabel.org/downloads/The-Wireless-Report-2014. pdf

Dogan, E.B., Bolderdijk, J.W. and Steg, L. (2014). Making small numbers count: Environmental and financial feedback in promoting eco-driving behaviours. *Journal of Consumer Policy* 37, 413–22. doi:10.1007/s10603-014-9259-z

Douglas, G. (n.d.). Help I want to save a life. Retrieved from http://www.graham-douglas.com/help-i-want-to-save-a-life/

Drinkaware (n.d.). Understand your drinking. Retrieved from https://www. drinkaware.co.uk/understand-your-drinking

Ebrahim, A. (2013, March 13). Let's be realistic about measuring impact [Blog post]. Retrieved from http://blogs.hbr.org/2013/03/lets-be-realistic-about-measur/

Ehrenberg, A.S. (1998). Repetitive advertising and the consumer. In J.P. Jones (ed.), *How advertising works: The role of research* (pp. 63–81). Thousand Oaks, CA: Sage.

Estonian Environmental Investment Center (2014). Ettepanekud keskkonnatead likkuse programmi rahastamis¬tingimuste kujundamiseks: Organisatsiooni töödokument [Propositions for the financing instruments of environmental education: Organisation's working document].

European Commission (n.d.). The policies. Retrieved from http://ec.europa.eu/policies/index_en.htm

European Commission (2014, September 2). Eco-innovation. When business meets the environment. Retrieved from http://ec.europa.eu/environment/eco-innovation/

European Environment Agency (n.d.). Environmental policy document catalogue. Retrieved from http://www.eea.europa.eu/policy-documents#c5=all&c0=10& b_start=0

European Social Innovation Competition (2014a). Urban Farm Lease. Retrieved from http://socialinnovationcompetition.eu/418/

European Social Innovation Competition (2014b). AutieCorp. Retrieved from http://socialinnovationcompetition.eu/392/

Evaluation Toolbox (n.d.). Problem tree / Solution tree analysis. Retrieved from http://evaluationtoolbox.net.au/index.php?option=com_content&view=article &id=28&Itemid=134

Evans, D., McMeekin, A. and Southerton, D. (2012). Sustainable consumption, behaviour change policies and theories of practice. *COLLeGIUM: Studies Across Disciplines in the Humanities and Social Sciences* 12, 113–29. Retrieved from https://helda.helsinki.fi/handle/10138/34226

Evans, N. (2012). A 'nudge' in the wrong direction. IPA Review 64, 16–19. Retrieved from https://ipa.org.au/publications/2129/a-'nudge'-in-the-wrong-direction

Ezzy, D. (2002). *Qualitative analysis: Practice and innovation.* New South Wales, Australia: Allen and Unwin.

Farrell, H. and Shalizi, C. (2011, November 9). 'Nudge' policies are another name for coercion. Retrieved from http://www.newscientist.com/article/mg21228376.500-nudge-policies-are-another-name-for-coercion.html#.VFZ4uskvCUU

Fisher, W.F. (1997). Doing good? The politics and antipolitics of NGO practices. *Annual Review of Anthropology* 26, 439–64. doi:10.1146/annurev.anthro.26.1.439

Flick, U. (2009). *An introduction to qualitative research* (4th ed.). London, England: Sage.

Foundation Centre (n.d.). Tools and resources for assessing social impact database. Retrieved from http://trasi.foundationcenter.org/

Future Learning Finland (n.d.). KiVa–Anti-bullying program. Retrieved from http://www.futurelearningfinland.fi/what-is-future-learning-finland/all-members/solution/kiva-anti-bullying-program

Gagnon, M., Jacob, J.D. and Holmes, D. (2010). Governing through (in)security: A critical analysis of a fear-based public health campaign. *Critical Public Health* 20, 245–56. doi:10.1080/09581590903314092

Gardner, J.R., Rachlin, R. and Sweeney, H.W.A. (1986). *Handbook of strategic planning.* New York, NY: John Wiley and Sons.

Geels, F.W. (2004). From sectoral systems of innovation to socio-techical systems. Insights about dynamics and change from sociology and institutional theory. *Research policy* 33, 897–920. doi:10.1016/j.respol.2004.01.015

Geels, F.W. (2005). The dynamics of transitions in socio-technical systems: A multi-level analysis of the transition pathway from horse-drawn carriages to automobiles (1860–1930). *Technology Analysis & Strategic Management* 17, 445–76. doi:10.1080/09537320500357319

Genco, S., Pohlmann, A. and Steidl, P. (2013). *Neuromarketing for dummies.* Mississauga, Canada: John Wiley & Sons Canada.

Giddens, A. (1984/1989). *The constitution of society: Outline of the theory of structuration.* Cambridge, England: Polity Press.

Giddens, A. (1991). *Modernity and self-identity. Self and society in the late modern age.* Stanford, CA: Stanford University Press.

Glarace, E.M., Ramanadhan, S. and Viswanath, K. (2011). Health information seeking. In T.L. Thompson, R. Parrott and J.F. Nussbaum (eds), *The Routledge handbook of health communication* (2nd ed.) (pp. 167–80). New York, NY: Taylor & Francis.

Gram-Hanssen, K. (2013). Efficient technologies or user behaviour, which is the more important when reducing households' energy consumption? *Energy Efficiency* 6, 447–57. doi:10.1007/s12053-012-9184-4

Gronow, J. (2009). Fads, fashions and 'real' innovations: Novelties and social change. In E. Shove, F. Trentmann and R. Wilk (eds), *Time, consumption and everyday life* (pp. 129–42). Oxford, England: Berg.

Habermas, J. (1981). New social movements. *Telos* 1981, 33–7. doi:10.3817/0981049033

Habermas, J. (1981/1987). *The theory of communicative action. Vol. 2. Liveworld and system: A critique of functionalist reason* (T.A. McCarthy, Trans.). Boston, MA: Beacon Press.

Halkier, B. (in press). Mundane science use in a practice theoretical perspective. A discussion of different understandings of the relations between citizen-consumers and public communication initiatives build on scientific claims. *Public Understanding of Science.*

Hanks, W.F. (1991/2003). Foreword by William F. Hanks. In J. Lave and E. Wenger (eds). *Situated learning. Legitimate peripheral participation* (pp. 13–24). Cambridge, England: Cambridge University Press.

Hanneman, R. and Riddle, M. (2005). *Introduction to social network methods.* Retrieved from http://faculty.ucr.edu/~hanneman/nettext/

Hanneman, R. and Riddle, M. (2011). Concepts and measures for basic network analysis. In J. Scott and P.J. Carrington (eds), *The Sage handbook of social network analysis* (pp. 340–69). Thousand Oaks, CA: Sage.

Hansen, P.G. and Jespersen, A.M. (2013). Nudge and the manipulation of choice: A framework for the responsible use of the nudge approach to behaviour change in public policy. *European Journal of Risk Regulation* 1, 3–28. Retrieved from http://www.lexxion.de/en/verlagsprogramm-shop/details/3099/33/ejrr/nudge-and-the-manipulation-of-choice

Hargreaves, T. (2011). Practice-ing behaviour change: Applying social practice theory to pro-environmental behaviour change. *Journal of Consumer Culture* 11: 1, 79–99. doi: 10.1177/1469540510390500

Harré, R. and van Langenhove, L. (eds). (1999). *Positioning theory: Moral contexts of intentional action.* Oxford, England: Blackwell.

Harries, T., Rettie, R., Studley, M., Burchell, K. and Chambers, S. (2013). Is social norms marketing effective?: A case study in domestic electricity consumption. *European Journal of Marketing* 47, 1458–75. doi:10.1108/EJM-10-2011-0568

Harvey, P.D. (1999). *Let every child be wanted: How social marketing is revolutionizing contraceptive use around the world.* Westport, CT: Auburn House.

HCT group (2013). Impact report 2013. Growing enterprise, growing impact. Retrieved from http://hctgroup.org/uploaded/hct-group-impact-report-2013.pdf

Healy, K. 2006. Do presumed consent laws raise organ procurement rates? *De Paul Law Review* 55, 1017–43. Retrieved from http://kieranhealy.org/files/papers/presumed-consent.pdf

Herlihy, P. (2002). *The alcoholic empire: Vodka and politics in late imperial Russia.* Oxford, England: Oxford University Press.

Hilton, M., McKay, J., Crowson, N. and Mouhot, J.-F. (2010, June 8). The big society: Civic participation and the state in modern Britain. Retrieved from http://www.historyandpolicy.org/papers/policy-paper-103.html

Hinsberg, L. (2011). Kampaania 'Kumm on seks!' vastuvõtt sihtrühmas [Reception of campaign 'Kumm on seks' in the target group] (Bachelor's thesis, University of Tartu, Tartu). Retrieved from http://hdl.handle.net/10062/25820

Hjarvard, S. (2008). The mediatization of society: A theory of the media as agents of social and cultural change. *Nordicom Review* 29, 105–34. Retrieved from http://www.nordicom.gu.se/sites/default/files/kapitel-pdf/269_hjarvard.pdf

Hornsby, A. (2012). *The good analyst. Impact measurement and analysis in the social-purpose universe*. London, England: Investing for Good.

Hota, M., Caceres, R.C. and Cousin, A. (2010). Can public-service advertising change children's nutrition habits? The impact of relevance and familiarity. *Journal of Advertising Research* 50, 460–77. doi:10.2501/S0021849910091610

Hove, T. (2009). The filter, the alarm system, and the sounding board: Critical and warning functions of the public sphere. *Communication and Critical/Cultural Studies* 6, 19–38. doi: 10.1080/14791420802632095

Innovation Network (n.d.). Logic model workbook. Retrieved from http://www.innonet.org/client_docs/File/logic_model_workbook.pdf

Inspiring Impact (n.d.). Impact hub. Retrieved from http://inspiringimpact.org/listings

Jackson-Webb, F. (2014, August 29). Plain packs don't drive smokers to buy cheap imports. Retrieved from http://theconversation.com/plain-packs-dont-drive-smokers-to-buy-cheap-imports-31013

Jones, J.P. (1998). Is advertising still salesmanship? In J.P. Jones (ed.), *How advertising works: The role of research* (pp. 82–95). Thousand Oaks, CA: Sage.

Juvonen, J. and Galván, A. (2008). Peer influence in involuntary social groups: Lessons from research on bullying. In M.J. Prinstein and K.A. Dodge (eds), *Peer influence processes among youth*. New York, NY: Guilford Press.

Kahn, M.E. and Morris, E.A. (2009). Walking the walk. The association between community environmentalism and green travel behavior. *Journal of the American Planning Association* 75, 389–405. doi:10.1080/01944360903082290

Kastner, I. and Matthies, E. (2014). Motivation and impact. Implications of a twofold perspective on sustainable consumption for intervention programs and evaluation designs. *GAIA 23,* 175–83. doi:10.14512/gaia.23.S1.5

Keller, M. and Halkier, B. (2014). Positioning consumption: A practice theoretical approach to contested consumption and media discourse. *Marketing Theory* 14, 35–51. doi:10.1177/1470593113506246

Keller, M. and Vihalemm, T. (2015). Struggling with the euro: Practical adaptation vs ideological resistance. In P. Strandbakken and J. Gronow (eds), *The consumer in society* (Manuscript submitted for publication). Oslo, Norway: Abstrakt.

King, A. (2000). Thinking with Bourdieu against Bourdieu: A 'practical' critique of the habitus. *Sociological Theory* 18, 417–33. doi:10.1111/0735-2751.00109

Kluger, R. (1996/1997). *Ashes to ashes: America's hundred-year cigarette war, the public health, and the unabashed triumph of Philip Morris.* New York, NY: Vintage Books.

Kohler-Koch, B. and Quittkat, C. (2013). *De-mystification of participatory democracy: EU-governance and civil society.* Oxford, England: Oxford University Press.

Kotler, P. and Levy, S.J. (1969). Broadening the concept of marketing. *Journal of Marketing* 33, 10–15. doi:10.2307/1248740

Kotler, P. and Lee, N. (2008). *Social marketing: Influencing behaviours for good* (3rd ed.). Los Angeles, CA: Sage.

Kozinets, R.V. (2010). *Netnography: Doing ethnographic research online.* London, England: Sage.

Krotz, F. (2007). The meta-process of 'mediatisation' as a conceptual frame. *Global Media and Communication* 3, 256–60. doi:10.1177/17427665070030 030103

Laitinen, K. (2012, October 4). KiVa: A research-based anti-bullying program [Presentation slides]. Retrieved from http://www.oph.fi/download/143565_ Kristiina_Laitinen_Pestalozzi_KiVa_04_10_2012.pdf

Lave, J. and Wenger, E. (eds). (1991/2003). *Situated learning. Legitimate peripheral participation.* Cambridge, England: Cambridge University Press.

Lavidge, R.J. and Steiner, G.A. (1961). A model for predictive measurements of advertising effectiveness. *Journal of Marketing* 25, 59–62. doi:10.2307/1248516

Lefebvre, C.R. (2013). *Social marketing and social change: Strategies and tools for improving health, well-being, and the environment.* San Francisco, CA: Jossey-Bass.

Livingstone, S. and Bober, M. (2005). UK children go online: Final report of key project findings. Retrieved from http://eprints.lse.ac.uk/399/

Livingstone, S., Lunt, S. and Miller, L. (2007). Citizens, consumers and the citizen-consumer: Articulating the citizen interest in media and communications regulation. *Discourse and Communication* 1, 63–89. doi:10.1177/ 1750481307071985

Lizardo, O. (2009). Is a 'special psychology' of practice possible? From values and attitudes to embodied dispositions. *Theory and Psychology* 19, 1–15. doi:10.1177/0959354309345891

Lizardo, O. and Strand, M. (2010). Skills, toolkits, contexts and institutions: Clarifying the relationship between different approaches to cognition in cultural sociology. *Poetics: Journal of Empirical Research on Culture, the Media and the Arts* 38, 204–27. doi:10.1016/j.poetic.2009.11.003

Lubi, K., Vihalemm, T. and Taba, P. (2014). Illness-related information seeking: The case of Parkinson's disease patients. In G. Lee (ed.), *Advances in education research* (Vols. 11–12) (pp. 98–111). Los Angeles, LA: Information Engineering Research Institute.

Madhavan, A. (2000). Market microstructure: A survey. *Journal of Financial Markets* 3, 205–58. doi:10.2139/ssrn.218180

Majchrzak, A., More, P. and Faraj, S. (2012). Transcending knowledge differences in cross-functional teams. *Organization Science* 23, 951–70. doi: 10.1287/orsc.1110.0677

Manoff, R.K. (1985). *Social marketing.* New York, NY: Praeger Publishers.

Mark, M. and Henry, G. (2006). Methods for policy-making and knowledge development evaluations. In I. Shaw, J. Greene and M. Mark (eds), *Handbook of evaluation: Policies, programs and practices* (pp. 317–39). Thousand Oaks, CA: Sage.

Martínez, B.R. (2009). Structure, power, and discourses of development in Spanish NGOs, *Nonprofit Management & Leadership* 20, 203–18. doi:10.1002/nml.249

Mayne, J. 2001. Addressing attribution through contribution analysis: Using performance measures sensibly. *Canadian Journal of Program Evaluation* 16, 1–24.

McDonald, S. (2005). Studying actions in context: A qualitative shadowing method for organizational research. *Qualitative Research* 5, 455–73. doi:10.1177/1468794105056923

McGregor, S.L.T. (2011). Complexity economics, wicked problems and consumer education. *International Journal of Consumer Studies* 36, 61–9. doi:10.1111/j.1470-6431.2011.01034.x

McGuire, A. (1999). How the tobacco industry continues to keep the home fires burning. *Tobacco Control* 8, 67–9. doi:10.1136/tc.8.1.67

Meroni, A. (ed.). (2007). Creative Communities. People inventing sustainable ways of living. Retrieved from https://archive.org/details/creative_communities

Mettler, S. (2011). *The submerged state. How invisible government policies undermine American democracy.* Chicago, IL: University of Chicago Press.

Morrison, B.E. and Vaandering, D. (2012). Restorative justice: Pedagogy, praxis, and discipline. *Journal of School Violence* 11, 138–55. doi:10.1080/15388220.2011.653322

Mouzelis, N. (2000). The subjectivist-objectivist divide: Against transcendence. *Sociology* 34, 741–62. doi:10.1177/S0038038500000456

Murray, R., Caulier-Grice, J. and Mulgan, G. (2010). The open book of social innovation. Retrieved from http://www.nesta.org.uk/sites/default/files/the_open_book_of_social_innovation.pdf

National Center for Chronic Disease Prevention and Health Promotion (Producer) (2011, July 22). The obesity epidemic [Video file]. Retrieved from http://www.cdc.gov/CDCTV/ObesityEpidemic/

National Fire Protection Association (n.d.). History. Retrieved from http://www.nfpa.org/safety-information/for-consumers/causes/smoking/coalition-for-fire-safe-cigarettes/history

National Water Safety Forum (2013). 2013 annual fatal incident report. Retrieved from http://www.nationalwatersafety.org.uk/waid/info/waid_fatalincidentreport_2013.xls

Nyborg, S. and Røpke, I. (2013). Constructing users in the smart grid – insights from the Danish eFlex project. *Energy Efficiency* 6, 655–70. doi: 10.1007/s12053-013-9210-1

O'Donohoe, S. (1994). Advertising uses and gratifications. *European Journal of Marketing* 28, 52–75. doi:10.1108/03090569410145706

Ölander, F. and Thøgersen, J. (2014). Informing versus nudging in environmental policy. *Journal of Consumer Policy* 37, 341–56. doi:10.1007/s10603-014-9256-2

Oosterveer, P.J.M. and Spaargaren, G. (2011). Organising consumer involvement in the greening of global food flows: The role of environmental NGOs in the case of marine fish. *Environmental Politics* 20, 97–114. doi:10.1080/0964401 6.2011.538168

Organization as Communication (n.d.). Webpage introducing the communicative constitution of organization. Retrieved from http://orgcom.wordpress.com

Orlikowski, W.J. (2010). The sociomateriality of organizational life: Considering technology in management research. *Cambridge Journal of Economics* 34, 125–41. doi:10.1093/cje/bep058

Paek, H.-J., Hove, T., Jeong, H.J. and Kim, M. (2011). Peer or expert? The persuasive impact of Youtube public service announcements producers. *International Journal of Advertising* 30, 161–88. doi:10.2501/IJA-30-1-161-188

Page, S.E. (2007). *The difference. How the power of diversity creates better groups, firms, schools, and societies.* Princeton, NJ: Princeton University Press.

Pathak, S. (2014, June 17). Nivea ad that turns into a kid-tracker wins mobile grand prix. Retrieved from http://adage.com/article/special-report-cannes-lions/nivea-ad-turns-kid-tracker-wins-mobile-grand-prix/293745/

Patton, M.Q. (2002). *Qualitative evaluation and research methods* (3rd ed.). Thousand Oaks, CA: Sage.

Phillips, L.J. (2011). *The promise of dialogue.* Amsterdam, The Netherlands: John Benjamins Publishing.

Policy Network on Flickr (2009, June 5). Anthony Giddens [Digital Image]. Retrieved from https://www.flickr.com/photos/35952250@N02/3597046763/

Putnam, L. and Mumby, D. (eds). (2014). *The Sage handbook of organizational communication.* London, England: Sage.

Putnam, R.D. (2000). *Bowling alone: The collapse and revival of American community.* New York, NY: Simon & Schuster.

Reckwitz, A. (2002). Toward a theory of social practices: A development in culturalist theorizing. *European Journal of Social Theory* 5, 243–63. doi:10. 1177/13684310222225432

Ricoeur, P. (1984–1988). *Time and narrative* (Vols 1–3) (K. McLaughlin and D. Pellauer, Trans.). Chicago, IL: University of Chicago Press.

Rimmer, M. (2013, February). Cigarettes will kill you: The High Court of Australia & plain packaging of tobacco products. Retrieved from http://www.wipo.int/wipo_magazine/en/2013/01/article_0005.html

Ristkok, M. (2014). Kohaliku toidu võrgustike sotsiaalsed praktikad [Social practices of local food networks] (Master's thesis, University of Tartu, Tartu, Estonia). Retrieved from http://dspace.utlib.ee/dspace/bitstream/handle/10062/42389/ristkok_maria_ma_2014.pdf?sequence=1

Roos, J.-P. (n.d.). Life politics: More than politics and life (style)? Retrieved from http://www.mv.helsinki.fi/home/jproos/sicinski.html

Roos, J.-P. and Hoikkala, N. (eds). (1998). *Elämänpolitiikka [Life politics]*. Helsinki, Finland: Gaudeamus.

Røpke, I. and Christensen, T.H. (2013). Transitions in the wrong direction? Digital technologies and daily life. In E. Shove and N. Spurling (eds), *Sustainable practices: social theory and climate change* (pp. 49–68). London, England: Routledge.

Ruckenstein, M., Suikkanen, J. and Tamminen, S. (2011). *Forget innovation. Focus on value creation*. Helsinki, Finland: Edita Publishing.

Sage (n.d.). Sage research methods. The essential online tool for researchers product (accessible via libraries, with access permit). Retrieved from http://www.sagepub.com/aboutSRMO.sp

Sahakian, M. and Wilhite, H. (2014). Making practice theory practicable: Towards more sustainable forms of consumption. *Journal of Consumer Culture* 14, 25–44. doi: 10.1177/1469540513505607

Salmivalli, C., Garandeau, C. and Veenstra, R. (2012). KiVa antibullying program: Implications for school adjustment. In G. Ladd and A. Ryan (eds), *Peer relationships and adjustment at school* (pp. 279–307). Charlotte, NC: Information Age Publishing.

Sapountzaki, K. (2010). Risk-reproduction cycles and risk positions in the social and geographical space. *Journal of Risk Research* 13, 411–27. doi:10.1080/13669871003629838

Saunders, M. (2011). Capturing effects of interventions, policies and programmes in the European context: A social practice perspective. *Evaluation* 17, 89–102. doi:10.1177/1356389010394480

Saunders, M., Trowler, P. and Bamber, V. (eds). (2011). *Reconceptualising evaluation in higher education: The practice turn*. New York, NY: McGraw-Hill.

Sayer, A. (2013). Power, sustainability and well being: An outsider's view. In E. Shove and N. Spurling (eds), *Sustainable practices: Social theory and climate change* (pp. 167–80). London, England: Routledge.

Schatzki, T.R. (1996). *Social practices: A Wittgensteinian approach to human activity and the social*. Cambridge, England: Cambridge University Press.

Schatzki, T.R. (1997). Practices and actions: A Wittgensteinian critique of Bourdieu and Giddens. *Philosophy of the Social Sciences* 27, 283–308. doi:10.1177/004839319702700301

Schatzki, T.R. (2002). *The site of the social. A philosophical account of the constitution of social life and change*. Pennsylvania, PA: Pennsylvania State University Press.

Schatzki, T.R. (2013). The edge of change: On the emergence, persistence, and dissolution of practices. In E. Shove and N. Spurling (eds), *Sustainable practices: Social theory and climate change* (pp. 31–46). London, England: Routledge.

Schwartz, B. (2010). An interview with Craig Lefebvre. *Social Marketing Quarterly* 16, 151–4. doi:10.1080/15245004.2010.526849

Schwartz, J. (2014, September 21). Rockefellers, heirs to an oil fortune, will divest charity of fossil fuels. Retrieved from http://www.nytimes.com/2014/09/22/us/heirs-to-an-oil-fortune-join-the-divestment-drive.html?module=Search&mabReward=relbias%3Aw

Scollo, M., Zacher, M., Durkin, S. and Wakefield, M. (2014). Early evidence about the predicted unintended consequences of standardised packaging of tobacco products in Australia: A cross-sectional study of the place of purchase, regular brands and use of illicit tobacco. *BMJ Open*, 4, e005873. doi:10.1136/bmjopen-2014-005873

Shove, E. (2010). Beyond the ABC: Climate change policy and theories of social change. *Environment and Planning A* 42: 6, 1273–85. doi:10.1068/a42282

Shove, E. and Pantzar, M. (2005). Consumers, producers and practices understanding the invention and reinvention of Nordic walking. *Journal of Consumer Culture* 5, 43–64. doi: 10.1177/1469540505049846

Shove, E., Pantzar, M. and Watson, M. (2012). *The dynamics of social practice. Everyday life and how it changes.* London, England: Sage.

Shove, E. and Spurling, N. (eds). (2013). *Sustainable practices: Social theory and climate change.* London, England: Routledge.

Shove, E. and Walker, G. (2014). What is energy for: Social practice and energy demand. *Theory, Culture & Society* 31, 41–58. doi:10.1177/0263276414536746

Social change (n.d.). In *Encyclopaedia Britannica*. Retrieved from http://www.britannica.com/EBchecked/topic/550924/social-change

Social impact (n.d.). In *BusinessDictionary*. (n.d.). Retrieved from http://www.businessdictionary.com/definition/social-impact.html

Social Impact Analysts Association (n.d.). Resources centre. Retrieved from http://www.siaassociation.org/resources/

Social Innovation Europe (n.d.). Webpage introducing European social innovation ideas and activities. Retrieved from http://www.socialinnovationeurope.eu/

Social Innovator (n.d.). Webpage introducing mainly U.S. social innovation ideas and activities. Retrieved from http://www.socialinnovator.info/

Southerton, D., McMeekin, A. and Evans, D. (2010). International review of behaviour change initiatives. Retrieved from http://www.scotland.gov.uk/Publications/2011/02/01104638/10

Spaargaren, G. and Oosterveer, P. (2010). Citizen-consumers as agents of change in globalizing modernity: The case of sustainable consumption. *Sustainability* 2, 1887–1908. doi:10.3390/su2071887

Spurling, N., McMeekin, A., Shove, E., Southerton, D. and Welch, D. (2013). Interventions in practice: Re-framing policy approaches to consumer behaviour.

Sustainable Practices Research Group Report. Retrieved from http://www. sprg.ac.uk/uploads/sprg-report-sept-2013.pdf

Stern, P. (2000). Toward a coherent theory of environmentally significant behavior. *Journal of Social Issues* 56: 3, 407–24.

Strategic design scenarios (n.d.). Webpage introducing strategic design ideas, possibilities and tools. Retrieved from http://www.strategicdesignscenarios. net/category/library-menu/

Stucker, C. (2006). *Mystery shopper's manual* (6th ed.). Sugar Land, TX: Special Interests Publishing.

Sulkunen, I. (1991). *History of the Finnish Temperance Movement.* Lewiston, NY: The Edwin Mellen Press.

Sulkunen, P. (2010). *The saturated society: Governing risk and lifestyles in consumer culture.* London, England: Sage.

Tago, M. (2014). Kuidas kujundada edukamaid keskkonnaalaseid sotsiaalse muutuse programme? [How to design more successful environmental social change programs?] (Master's thesis, University of Tartu, Tartu). Retrieved from http://dspace.utlib.ee/dspace/bitstream/handle/10062/42391/tago_maril iis_ma_2014.pdf?sequence=1

Thaler, R.H. and Sunstein, C. R. (2008). *Nudge. Improving decisions about health, wealth, and happiness.* New Haven, CT: Yale University Press.

The Economist (2010, August 12). Social innovation. Let's hear those ideas. Retrieved from www.economist.com/node/16789766

The Global Value Exchange (n.d.). The webpage of the Global Value Exchange. Retrieved from http://globalvaluexchange.org

The SROI Network (n.d.). The webpage of the SROI Network. Retrieved from http://www.thesroinetwork.org

The Young Foundation (n.d.). Webpage introducing the Young Foundation. Retrieved from http://youngfoundation.org/

Tomlinson, M. and McMeekin, A. (2001). The evolution of consumption routines. In A. McMeekin, K. Green, M. Tomlinson and V. Walsh (eds), *Innovation by demand: Interdisciplinary approaches to the study of demand and its role in innovation.* Manchester, England: University Press.

Trentmann, F. (2007). Citizenship and consumption. *Journal of Consumer Culture* 7, 147–58. doi:10.1177/1469540507077667

Trink, E. (2015). Veeohutuskampaania mõju praktikapõhine mõõtmine [Practice-based measurement of the effect of water safety campaign]. Manuscript in preparation, Institute of Social Studies, University of Tartu, Tartu, Estonia.

UK Department of Health (n.d.). Alcohol labelling. Retrieved from https:// responsibilitydeal.dh.gov.uk/pledges/pledge/?pl=1

Umpfenbach, K. (2014) Influences on consumer behaviour. Policy implications beyond nudging. *Ecologic Institute, Berlin.* Retrieved from http://ec.europa. eu/environment/enveco/economics_policy/pdf/Behaviour%20Policy%20 Brief.pdf

Vihalemm, T. and Keller M. (2013, August). Media and the complexities of everyday life: Studying audience with practice theory and positioning analysis [Conference paper]. Retrieved from: http://www.esa11thconference.eu/skins/default/static/ESA_2013_Abstract_Book.pdf

Vihalemm, T., Kiisel, M. and Harro-Loit, H. (2012). Citizens' response patterns to warning messages. *Journal of Contingencies and Crisis Management* 20, 13–25. doi:10.1111/j.1468-5973.2011.00655.x

Warde, A. (2013). What sort of a practice is eating? In E. Shove and N. Spurling (eds), *Sustainable practices: Social theory and climate change* (pp. 17–30). London, England: Routledge.

Warde, A. and Southerton, D. (eds) (2012a). *The habits of consumption.* Helsinki, Finland: Helsinki Collegium for Advanced Studies.

Warde, A. and Southerton, D. (2012b). Introduction. In A. Warde and D. Southerton (eds), *The habits of consumption* (pp. 1–24). Helsinki, Finland: Helsinki Collegium for Advanced Studies.

Weinreich, N.K. (n.d.). What is social marketing? Retrieved from http://www.social-marketing.com/Whatis.html

Weiss, C.H. (1972). *Evaluation research. Methods for assessing program effectiveness.* Englewood Cliffs, NJ: Prentice-Hall.

Wenger, E. (1998). *Communities of practice. Learning, meaning, and identity.* J.S. Brown, R. Pea, C. Heath and L.A. Suchman (eds). Cambridge, England: Cambridge University Press.

Western Organization of Resource Councils. (2010). How to work in coalitions. Retrieved from http://www.worc.org/userfiles/file/Publications/Work_in_Coalitions.pdf

Whitford, J. (2002). Pragmatism and the untenable dualism of means and ends: Why rational choice theory does not deserve paradigmatic privilege. *Theory and Society* 31, 325–63. doi:10.1023/A:1016232404279

Wilson, L.J. and Ogden, J.D. (2008). *Strategic communications planning for effective public relations and marketing.* Dubuque, IA: Kendall Hunt.

Wilson, S. (2013, April 25). UK Responsibility Deal pledge on alcohol unit reduction [Presentation slides]. Retrieved from http://ec.europa.eu/health/alcohol/docs/ev_20130425_co07_en.pdf

Wolff, F. and Schönherr, N. (2011). The impact evaluation of sustainable consumption policy instruments. *Journal of Consumer Policy* 34, 43–66. doi:10.1007/s10603-010-9152-3

Worksheet Works (n.d.). Graphic organizers. Retrieved from http://www.worksheetworks.com/miscellanea/graphic-organizers.html

World Health Organization (n.d.). Policy documents. Retrieved from http://www.who.int/hrh/documents/policy/en/

World Health Organization (2014, April). Drowning (No. 347) [Fact sheet]. Retrieved from http://www.who.int/mediacentre/factsheets/fs347/en/

Yrityskylä (2014, November 6). What is Me & MyCity. Retrieved from http://yrityskyla.fi/en/me-mycity/

Index

For Product Safety Concerns and Information please contact our EU
representative GPSR@taylorandfrancis.com Taylor & Francis Verlag GmbH,
Kaufingerstraße 24, 80331 München, Germany

Printed and bound by CPI Group (UK) Ltd, Croydon, CR0 4YY

01/05/2025

01858422-0006